JAZZ PIANO SOLOS VOLUME 36

broadway jazz

Arranged by Brent Edstrom

contents

ISBN 978-1-4950-1730-8

HAL•LEONARD®
7777 W. BLUEMOUND RD. P.O. BOX 13819 MILWAUKEE, WI 53213

Visit Hal Leonard Online at
www.halleonard.com

ALL THE THINGS YOU ARE

from VERY WARM FOR MAY

Lyrics by OSCAR HAMMERSTEIN II
Music by JEROME KERN

Bright Latin

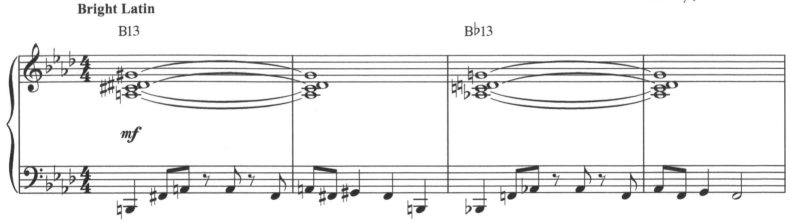

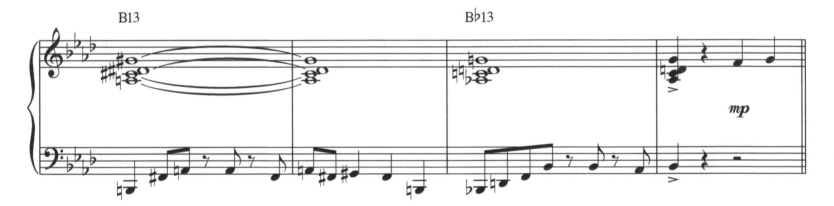

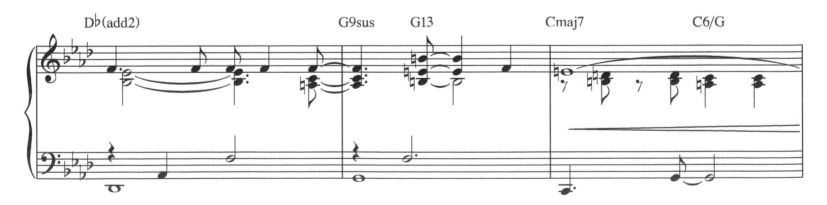

3

Cmaj7 Cm7 Fm7

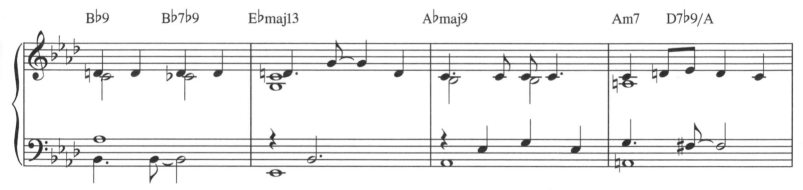

Bb9 Bb7b9 Ebmaj13 Abmaj9 Am7 D7b9/A

Gmaj9 D9sus

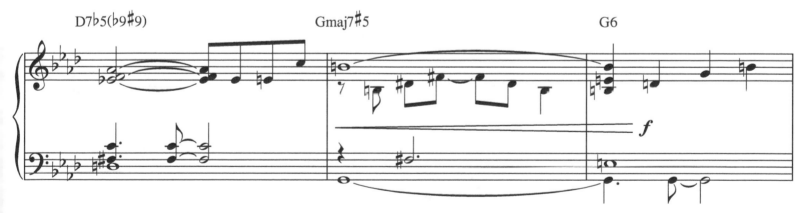

D7b5(b9#9) Gmaj7#5 G6

F#m7b5 B7b9 Emaj7#11 C7#5(#9) C9#5 C7#5(b9)

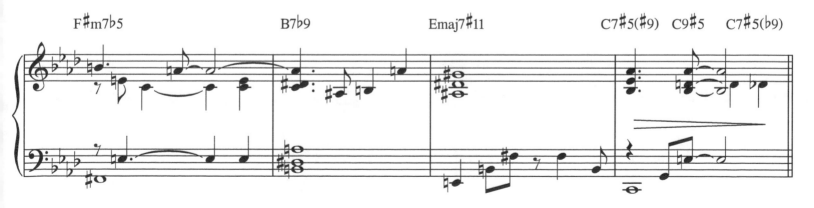

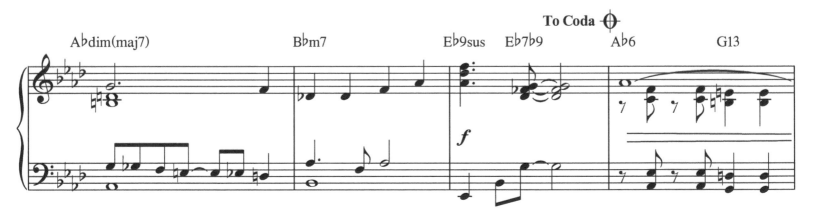

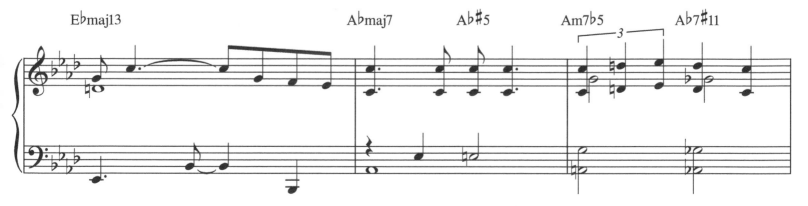

BODY AND SOUL
from THREE'S A CROWD

Words by EDWARD HEYMAN,
ROBERT SOUR and FRANK EYTON
Music by JOHN GREEN

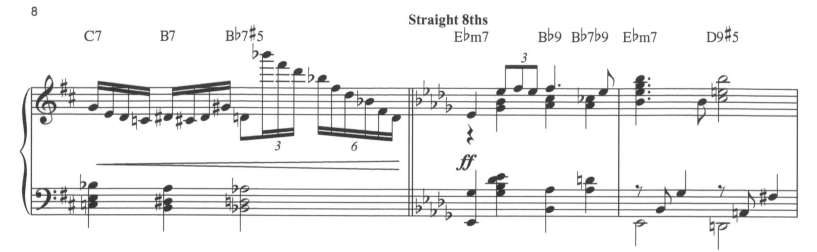

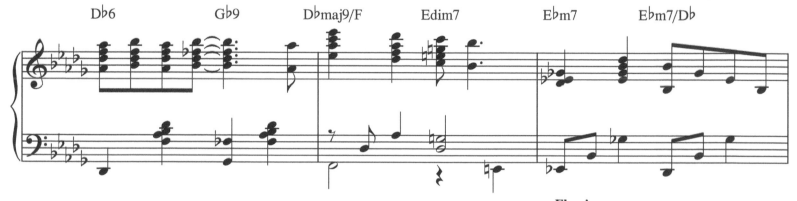

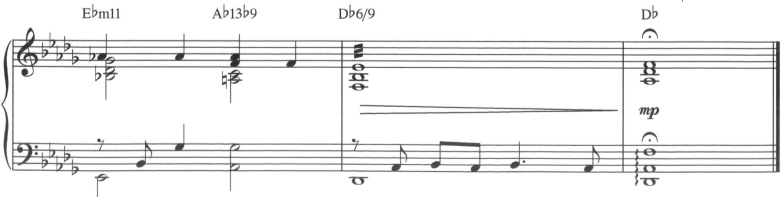

I COULD WRITE A BOOK

from PAL JOEY

Words by LORENZ HART
Music by RICHARD RODGERS

Moderate Swing

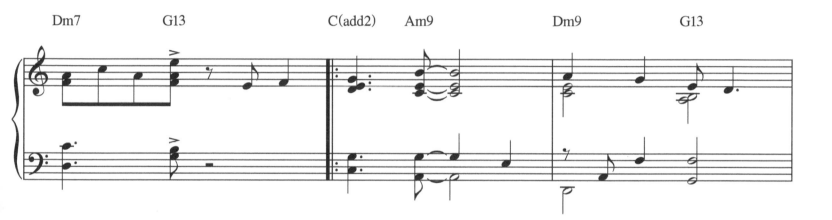

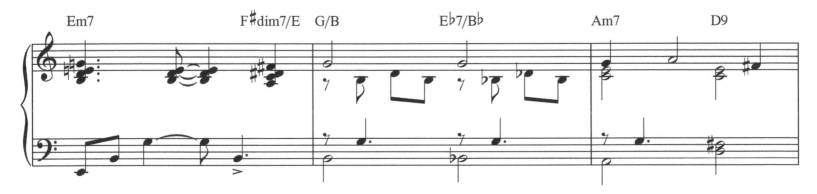

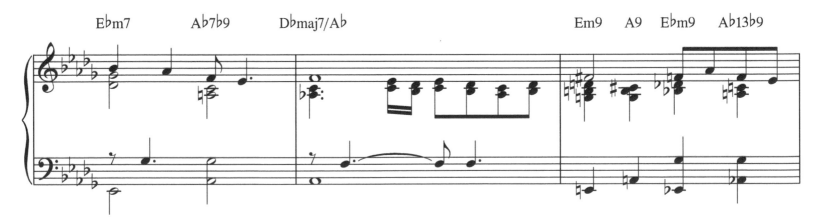

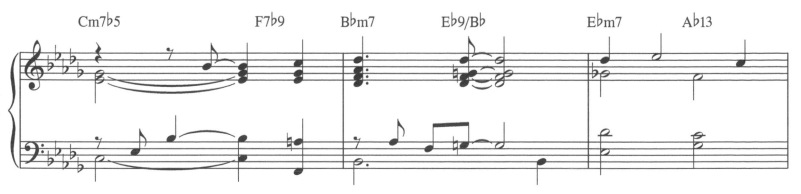

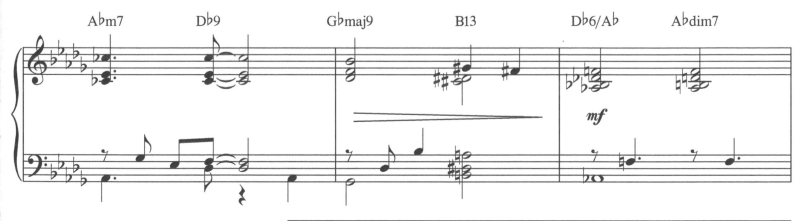

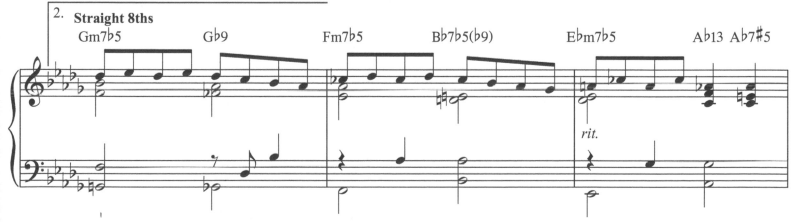

FALLING IN LOVE WITH LOVE

from THE BOYS FROM SYRACUSE

Words by LORENZ HART
Music by RICHARD RODGERS

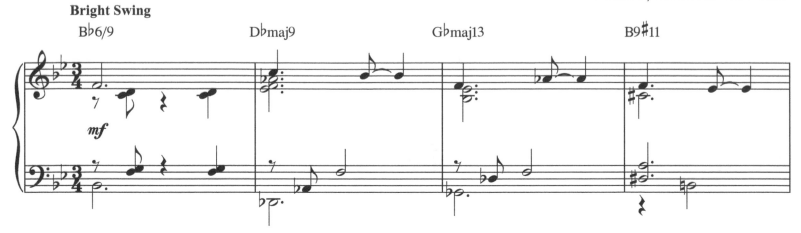

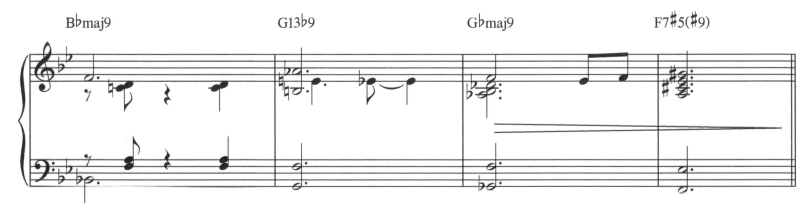

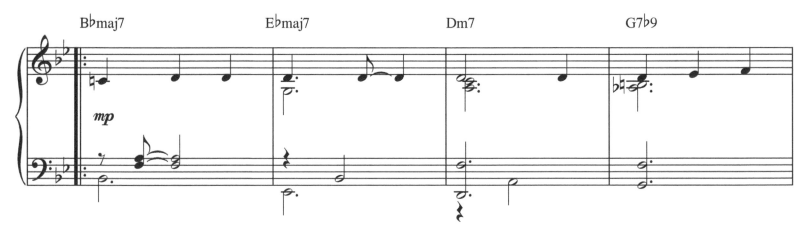

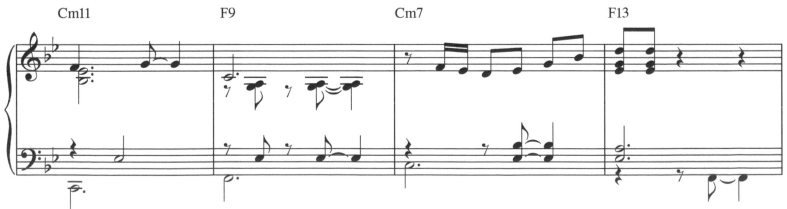

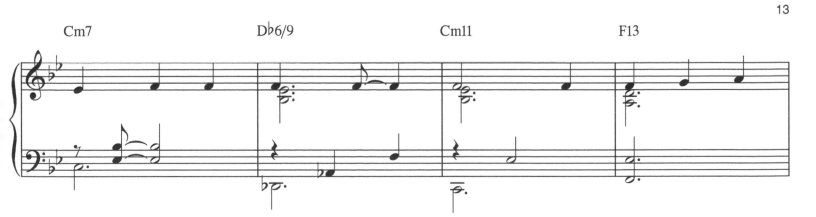

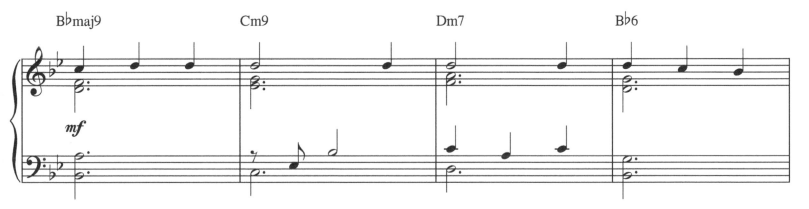

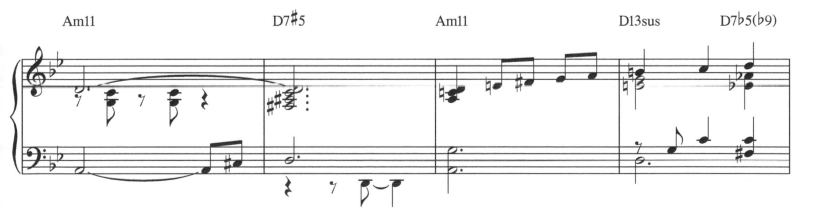

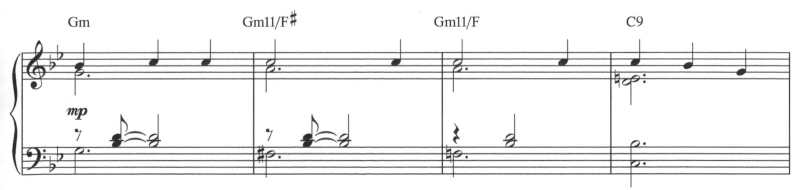

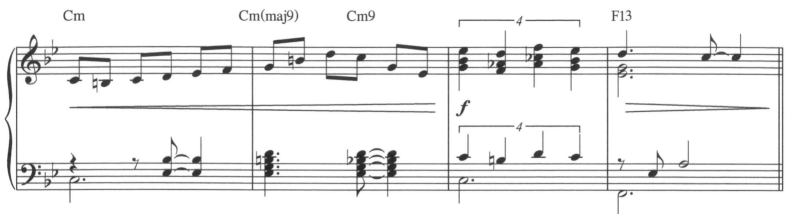

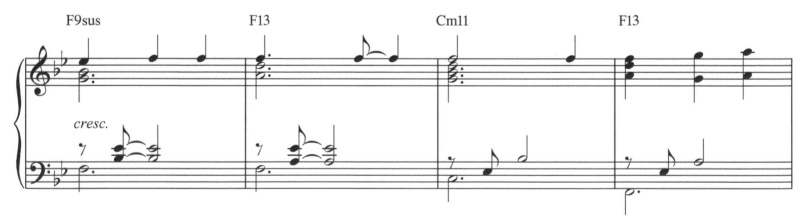

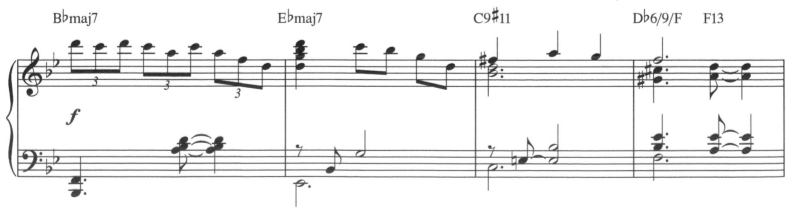

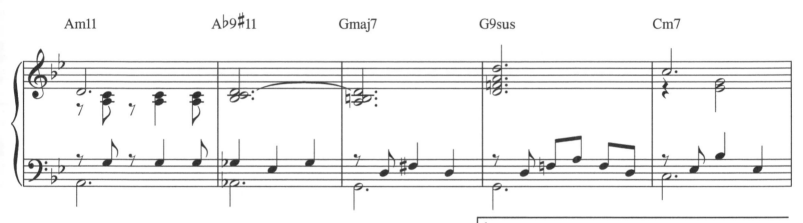

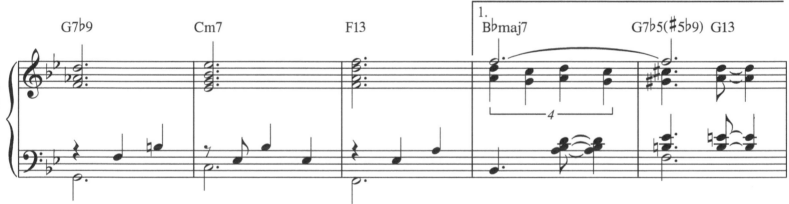

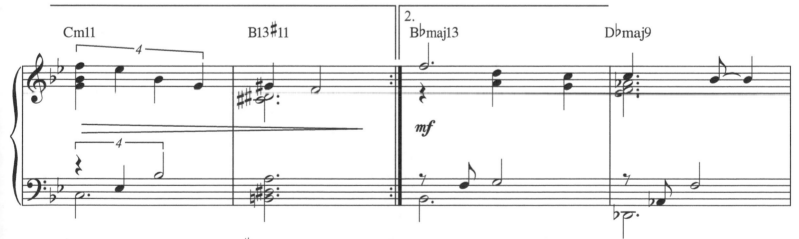

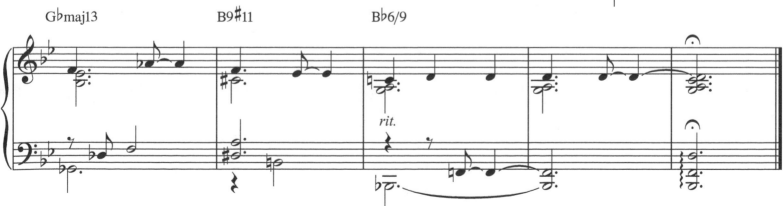

I LOVE YOU
from MEXICAN HAYRIDE

Words and Music by
COLE PORTER

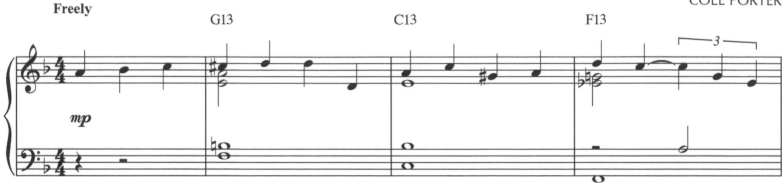

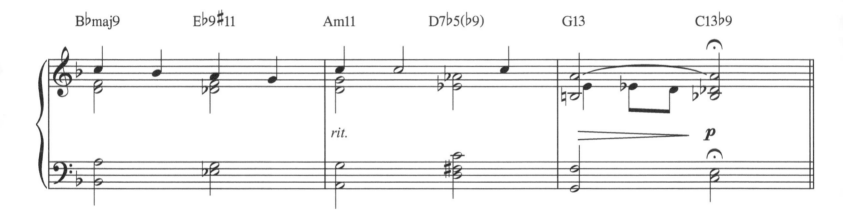

Bright Rhumba

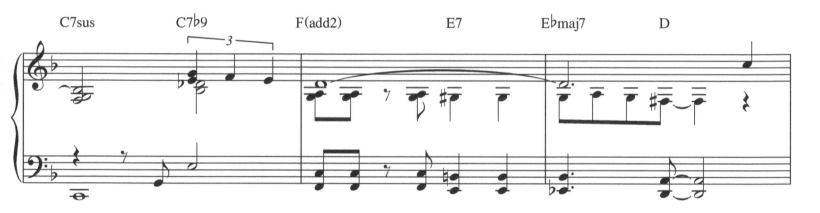

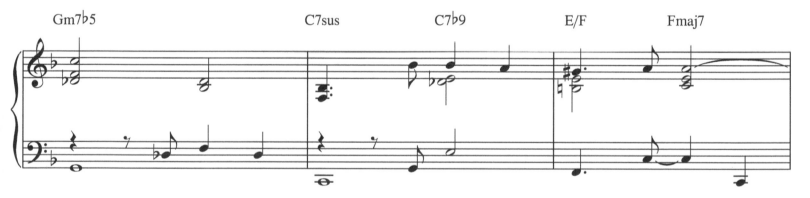

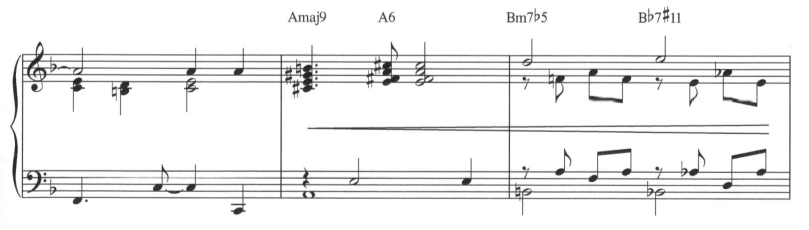

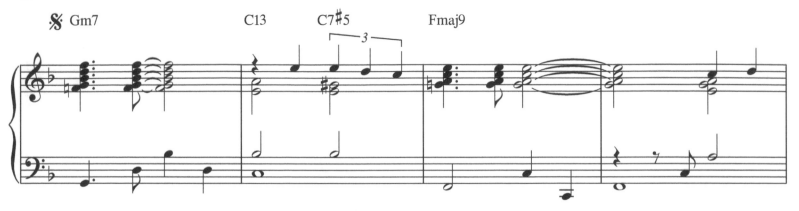

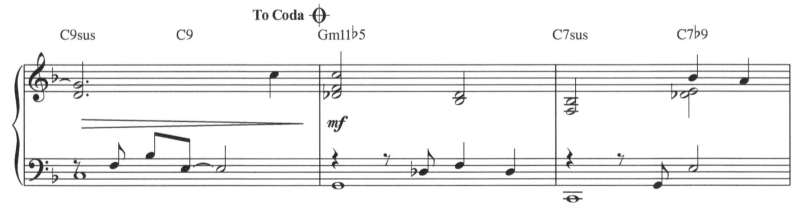

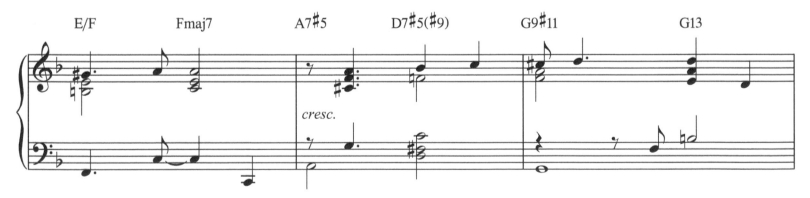

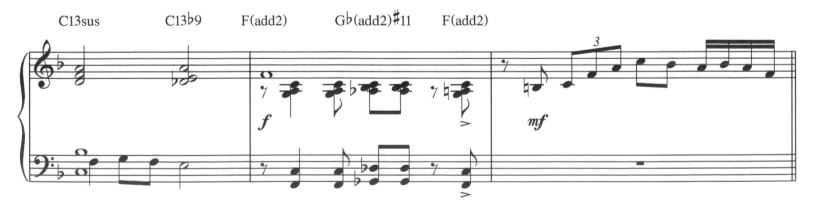

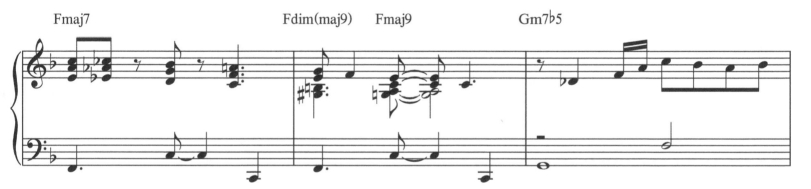

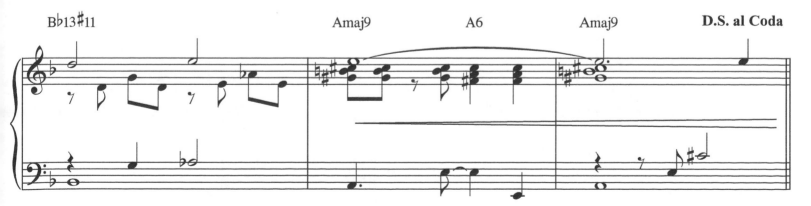

20

CODA

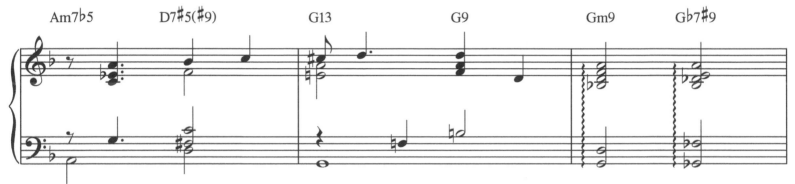

IF EVER I WOULD LEAVE YOU
from CAMELOT

Words by ALAN JAY LERNER
Music by FREDERICK LOEWE

Moderate Latin

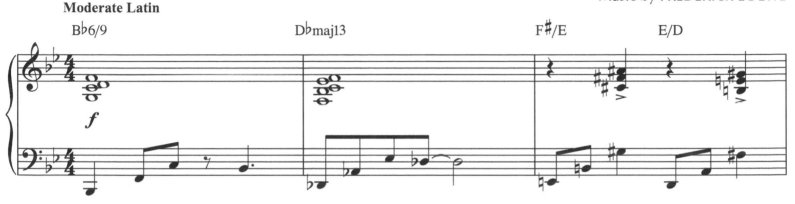

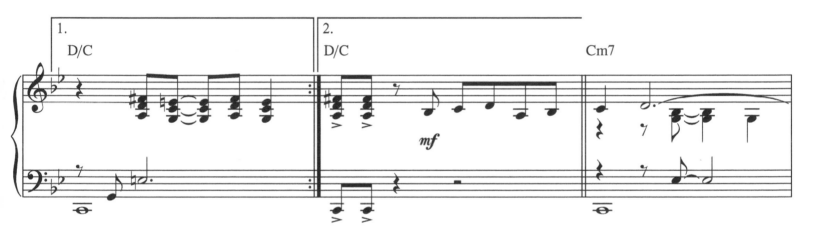

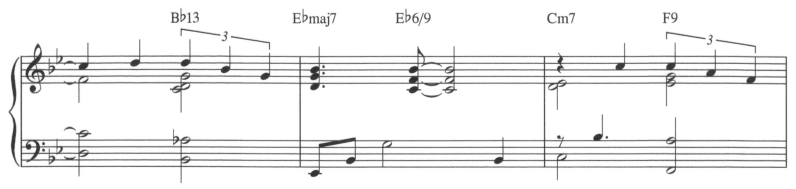

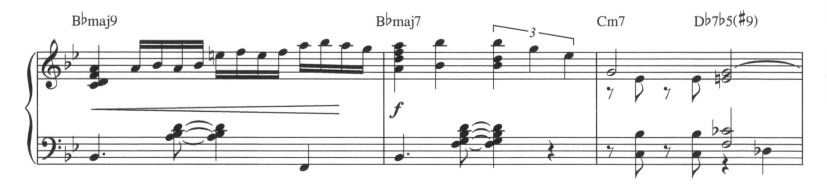

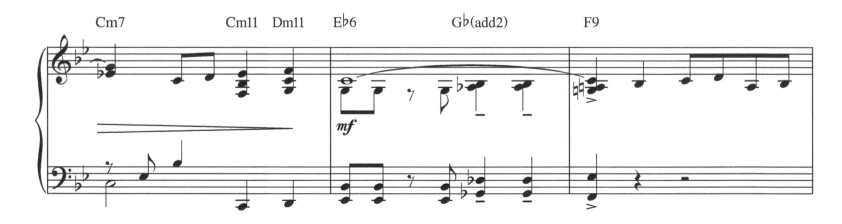

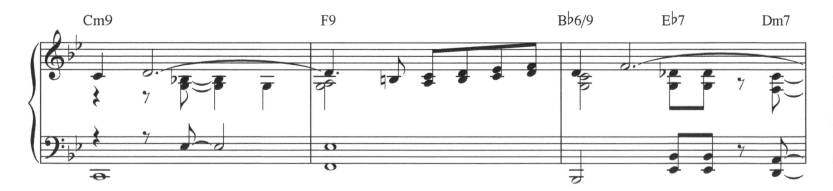

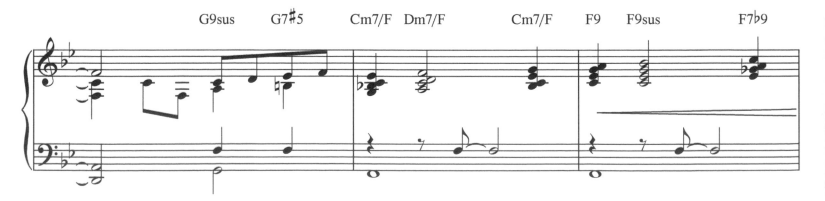

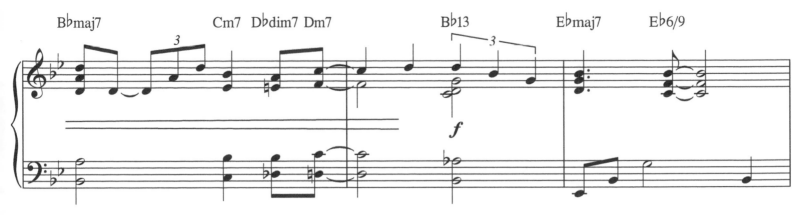

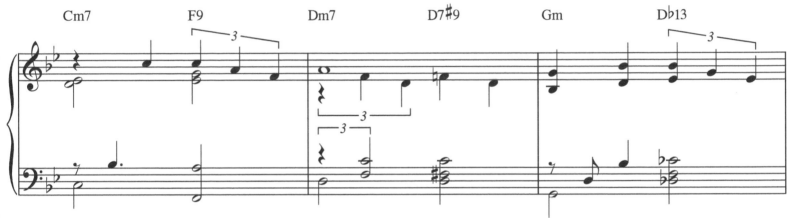

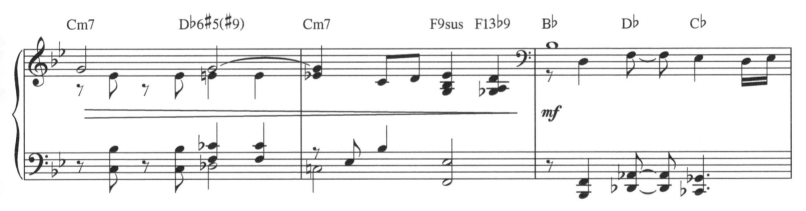

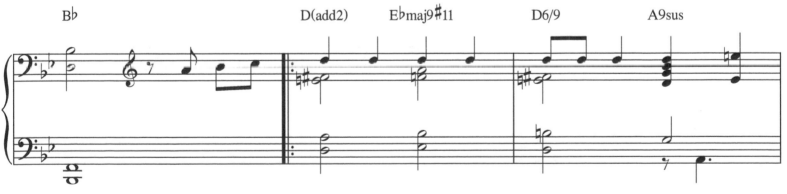

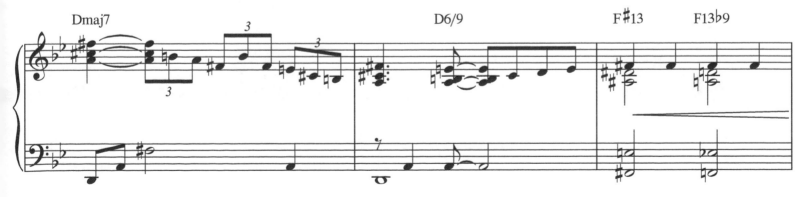

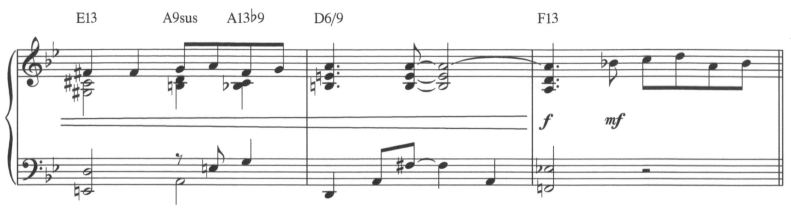

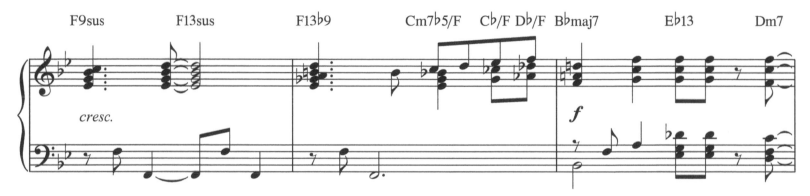

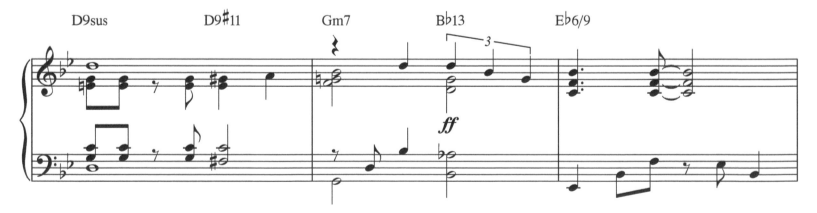

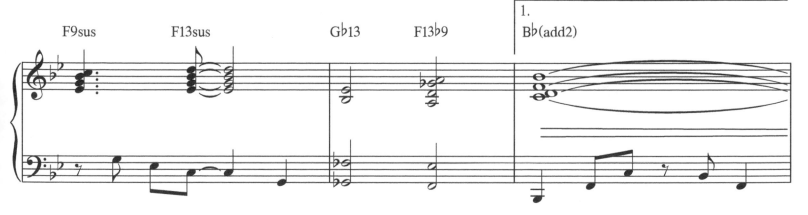

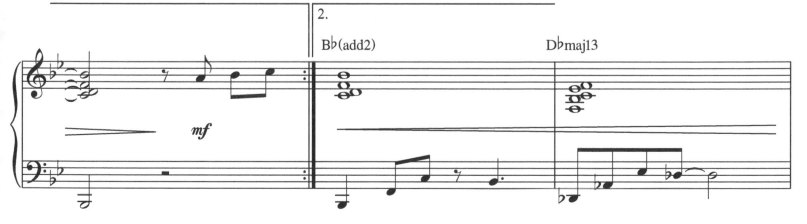

IF I WERE A BELL

from GUYS AND DOLLS

By FRANK LOESSER

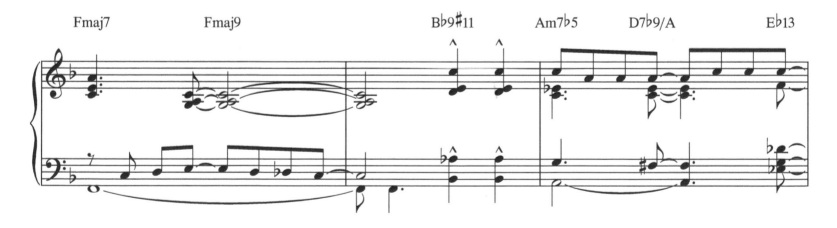

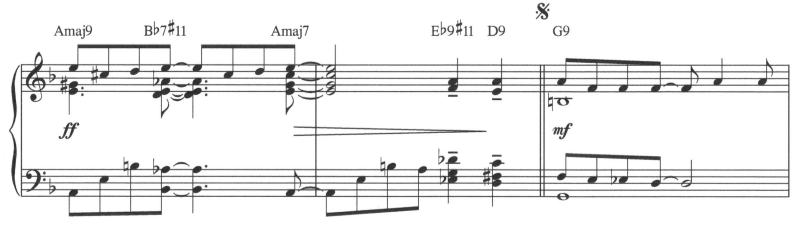

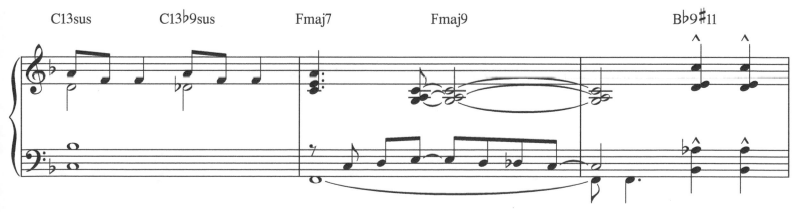

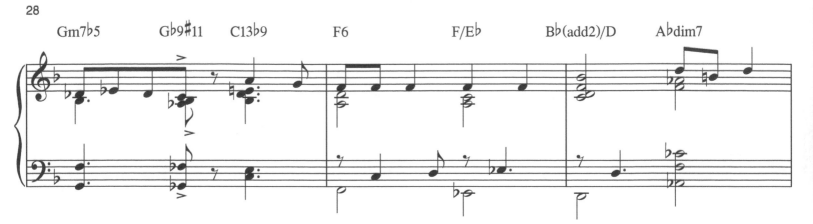

To Coda ⊕

LITTLE GIRL BLUE

from JUMBO

Words by LORENZ HART
Music by RICHARD RODGERS

Freely

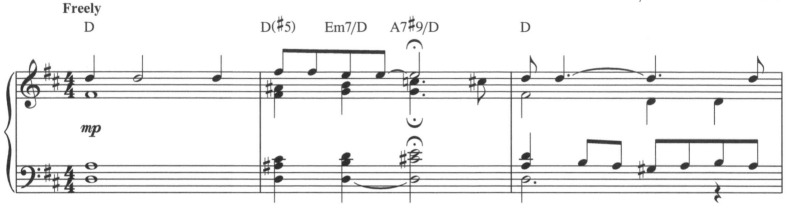

Arrangement based on one by Oscar Peterson

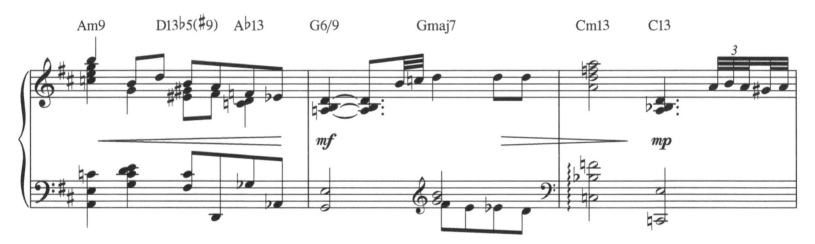

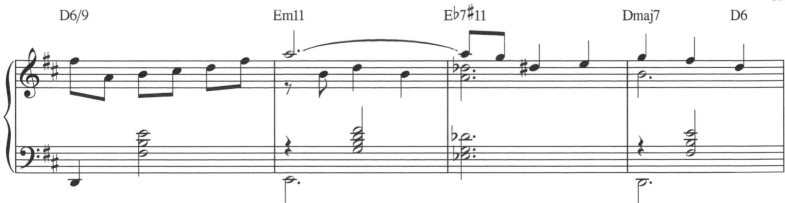

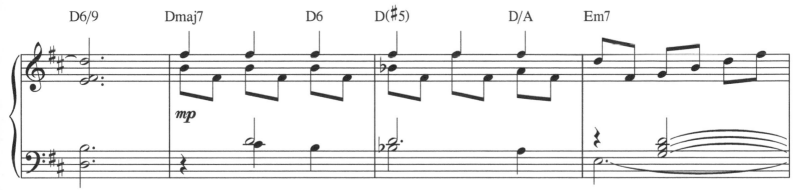

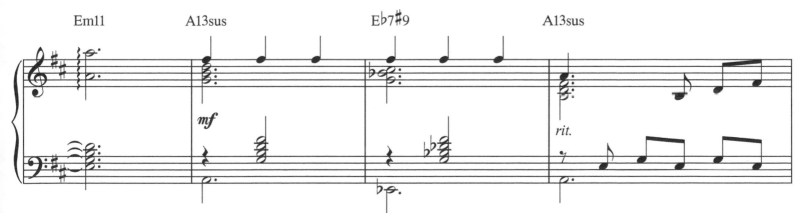

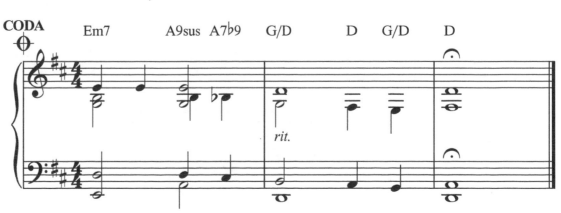

LULLABY OF BROADWAY

from GOLD DIGGERS OF 1935
from 42ND STREET

Words by AL DUBIN
Music by HARRY WARREN

Moderately slow Swing

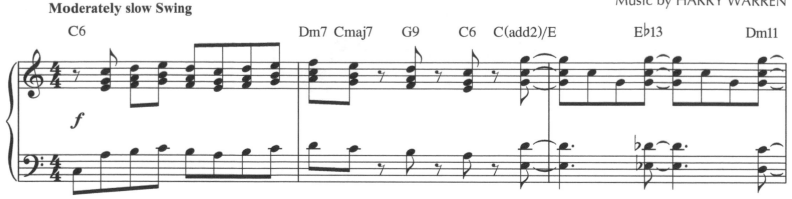

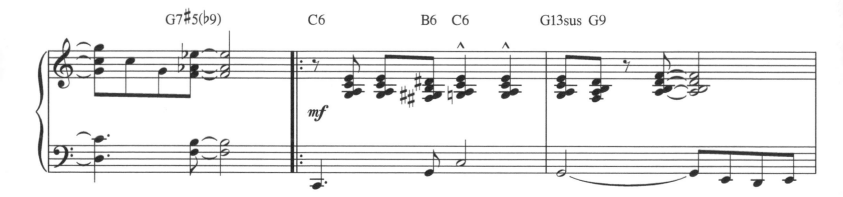

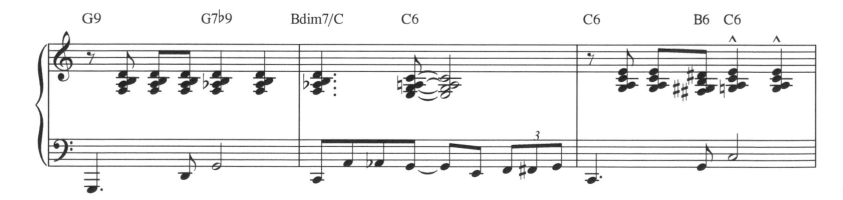

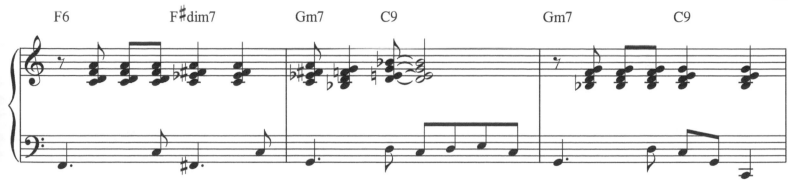

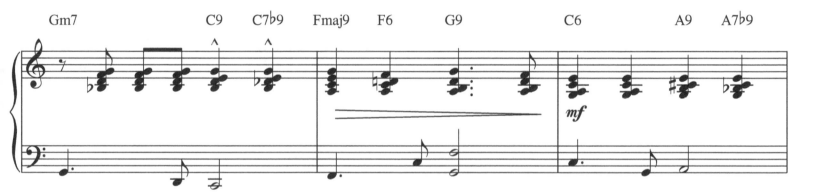

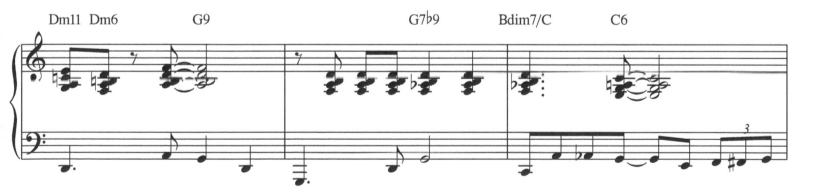

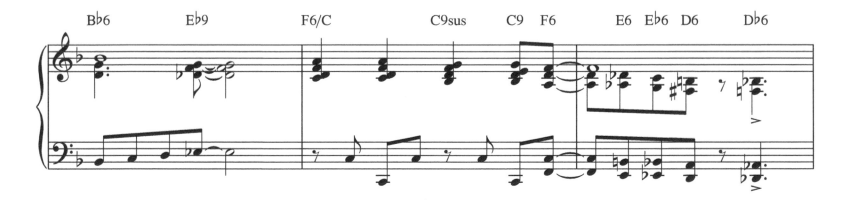

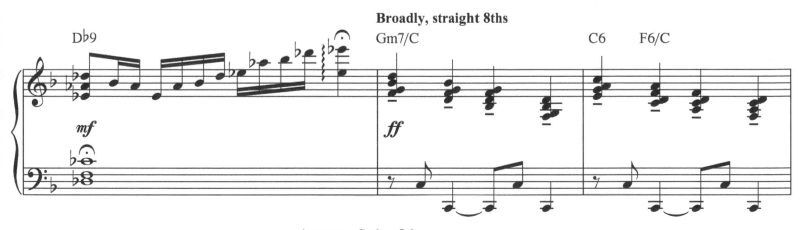

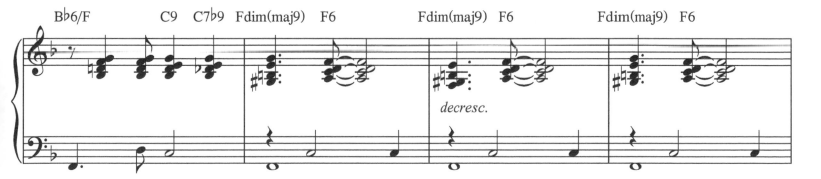

MAKE SOMEONE HAPPY
from DO RE MI

Words by BETTY COMDEN
and ADOLPH GREEN
Music by JULE STYNE

Moderate Swing

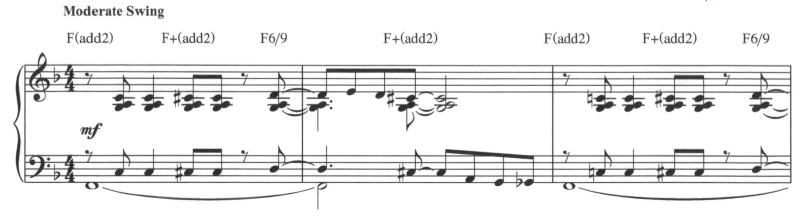

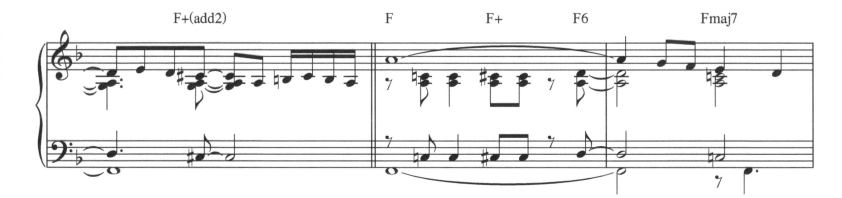

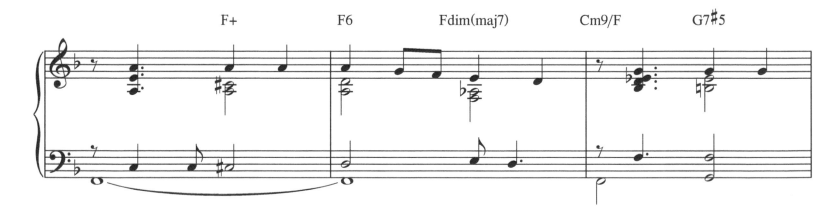

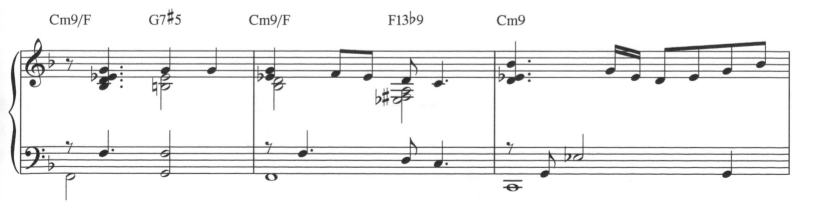

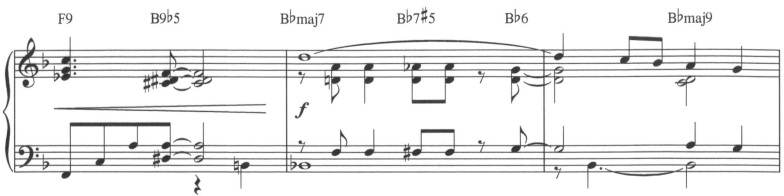

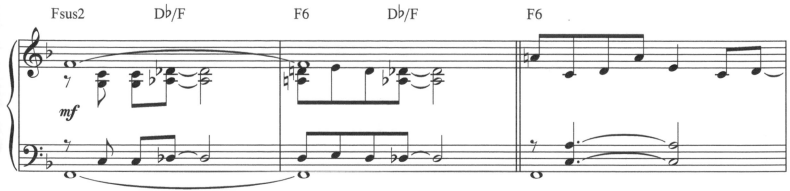

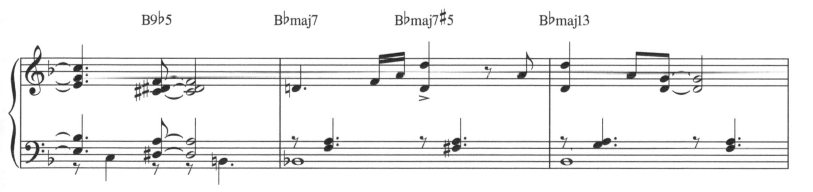

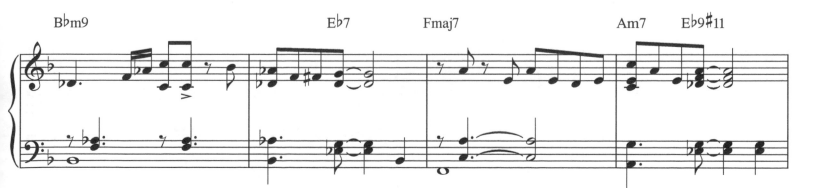

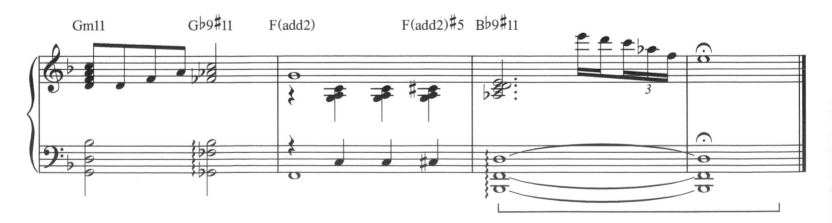

MY FUNNY VALENTINE
from BABES IN ARMS

Words by LORENZ HART
Music by RICHARD RODGERS

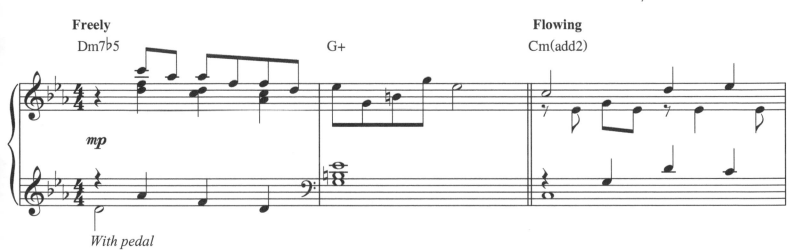

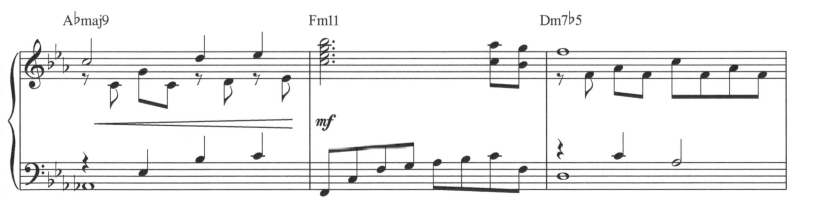

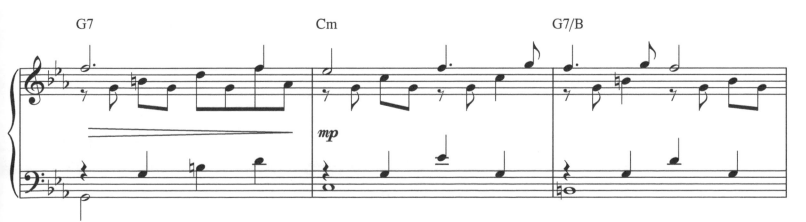

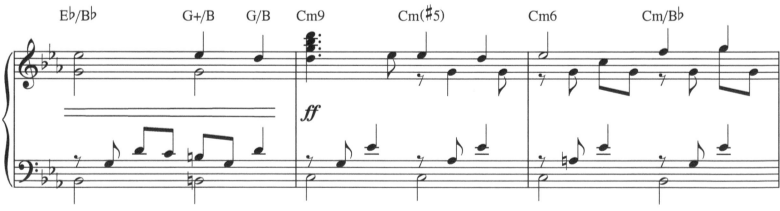

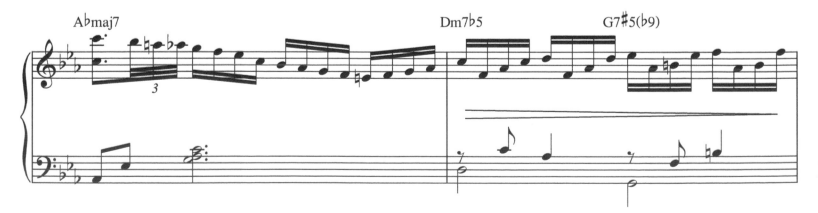

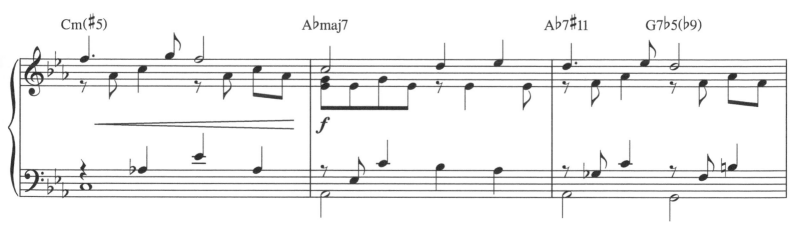

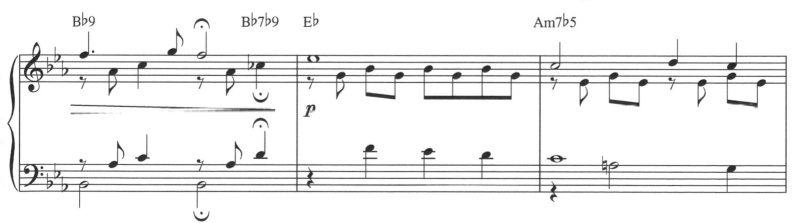

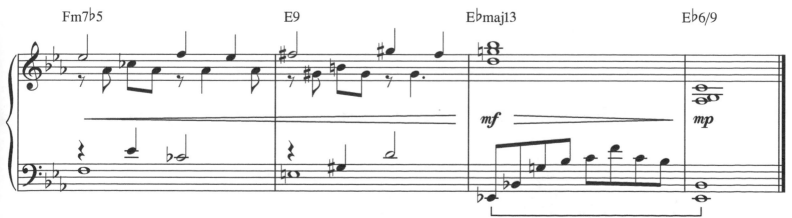

MY ROMANCE

from JUMBO

Words by LORENZ HART
Music by RICHARD RODGERS

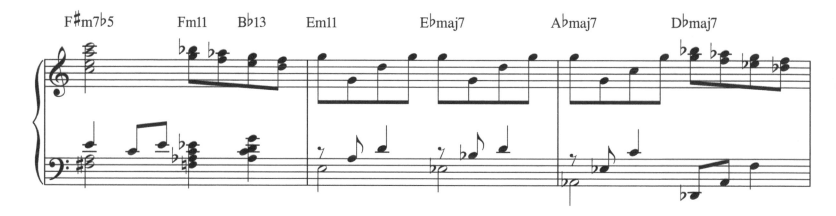

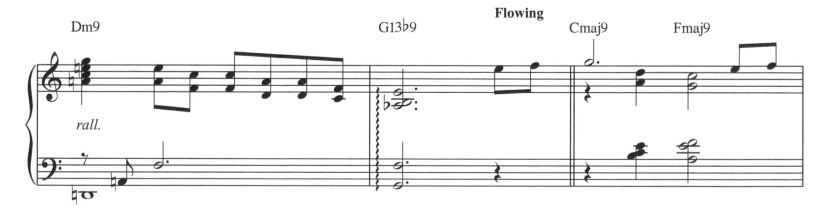

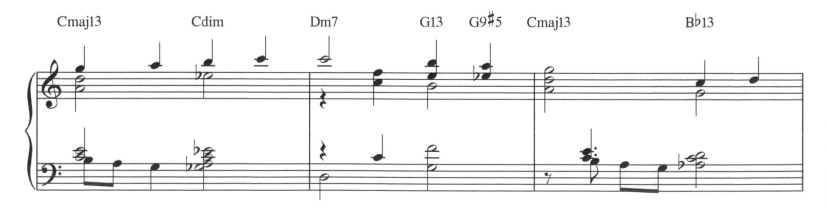

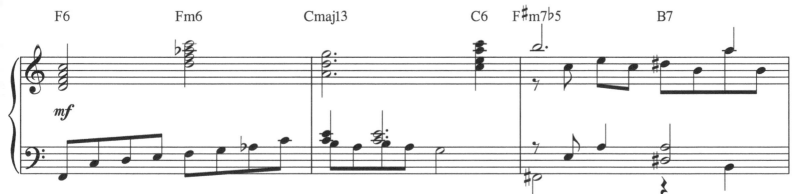

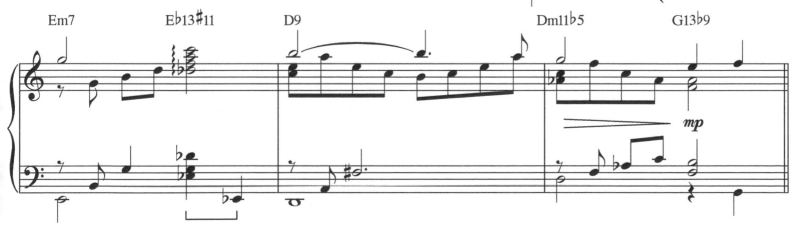

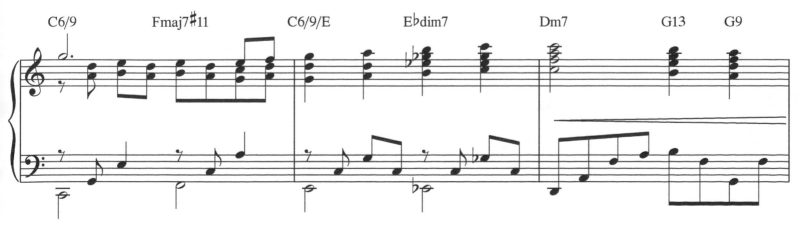

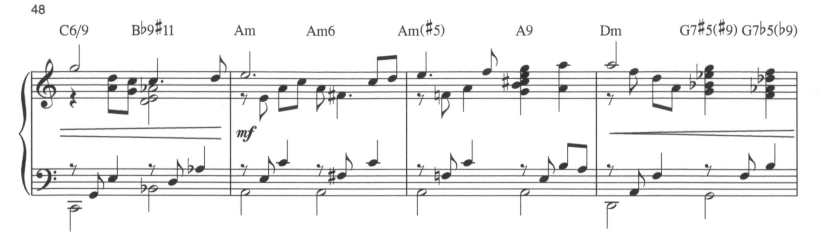

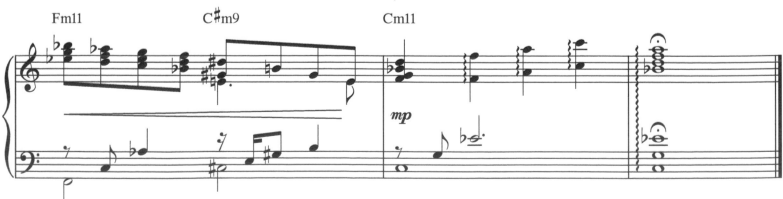

ON THE STREET WHERE YOU LIVE

from MY FAIR LADY

Words by ALAN JAY LERNER
Music by FREDERICK LOEWE

Moderate Swing

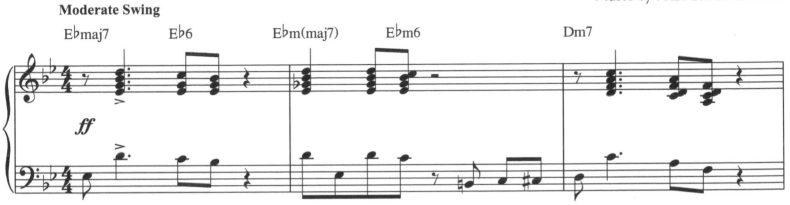

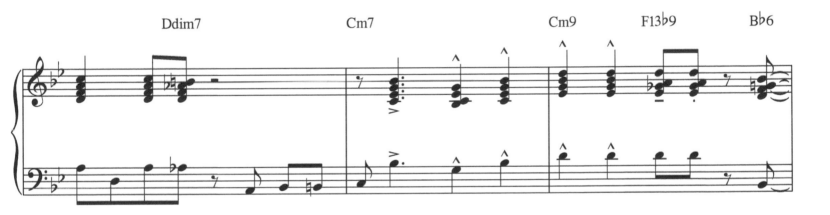

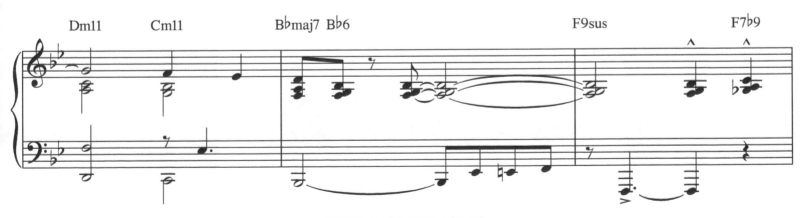

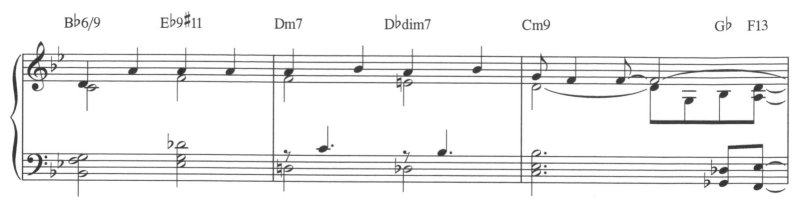

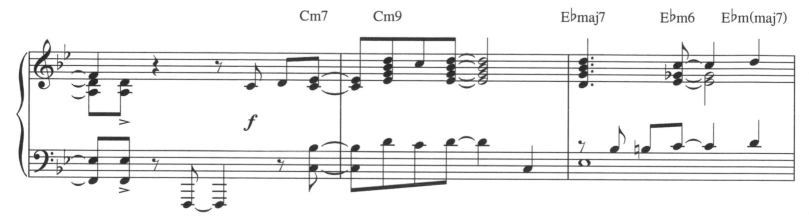

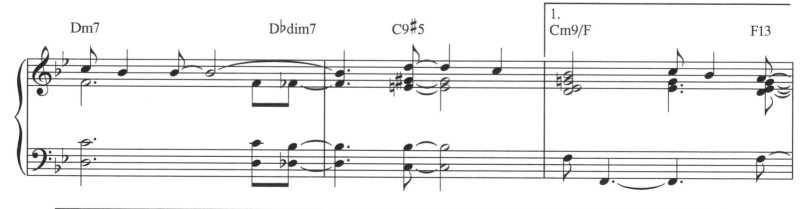

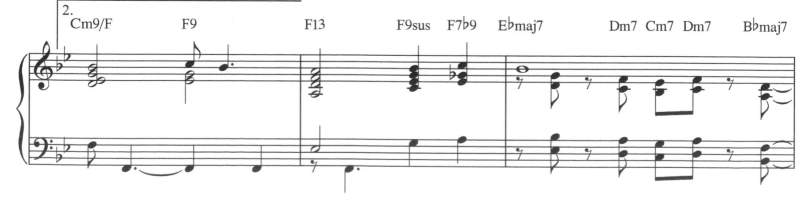

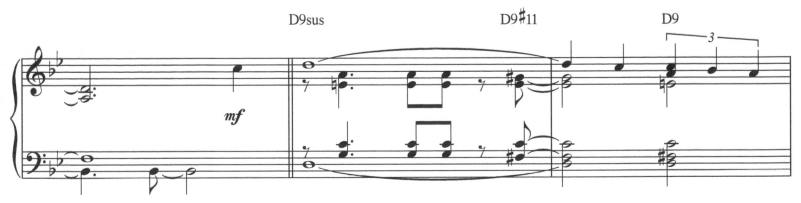

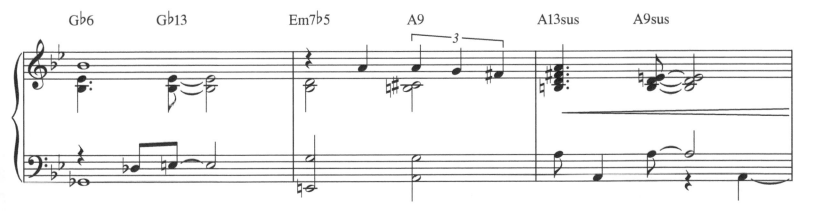

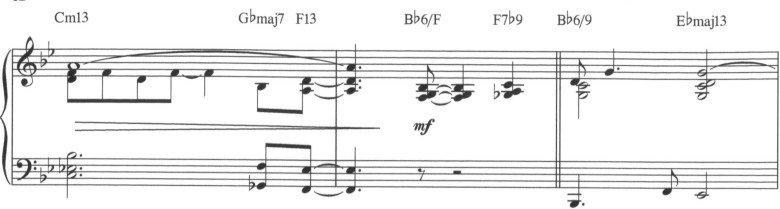

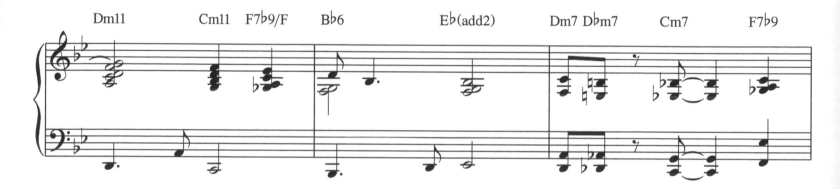

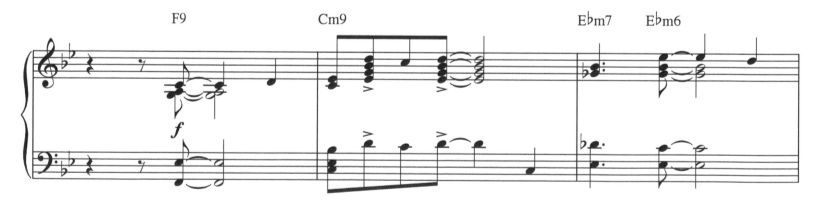

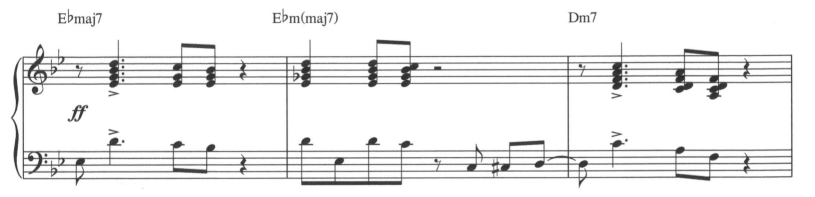

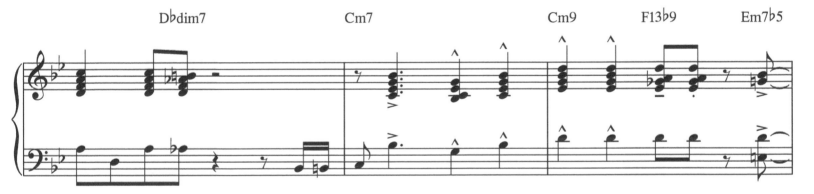

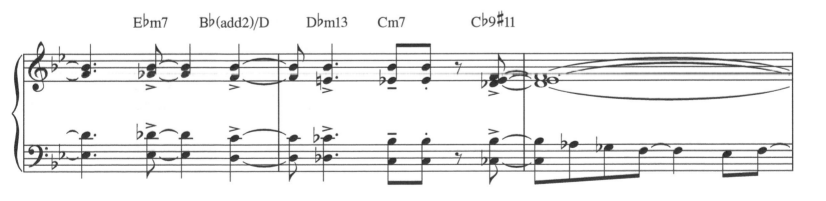

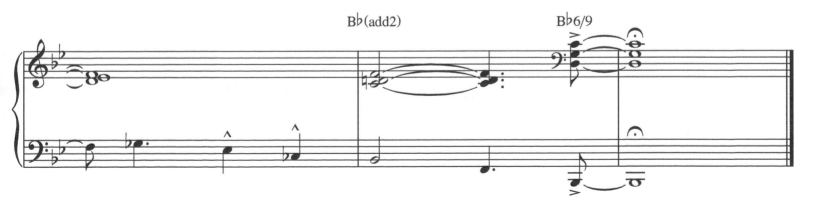

OLD DEVIL MOON
from FINIAN'S RAINBOW

Words by E.Y. "YIP" HARBURG
Music by BURTON LANE

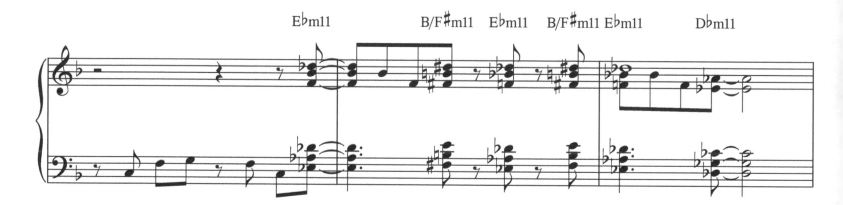

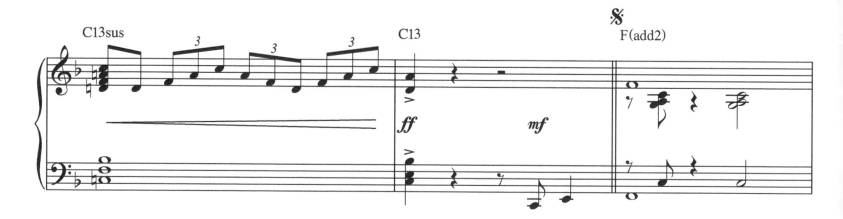

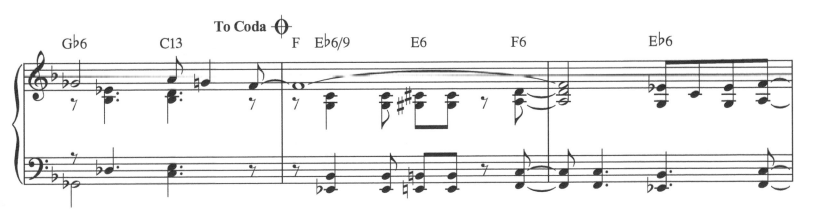

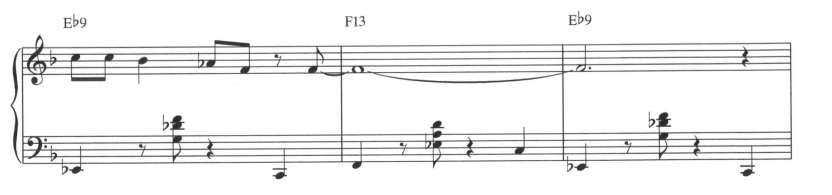

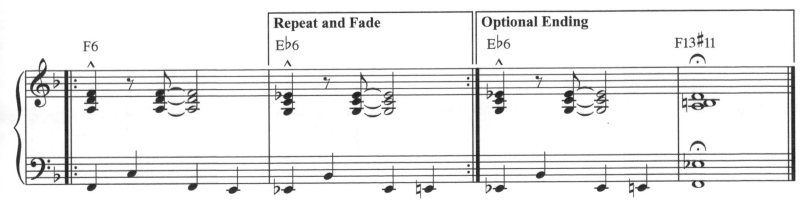

ON A CLEAR DAY
(You Can See Forever)
from ON A CLEAR DAY YOU CAN SEE FOREVER

Words by ALAN JAY LERNER
Music by BURTON LANE

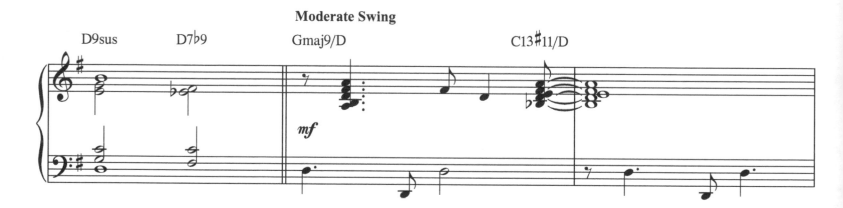

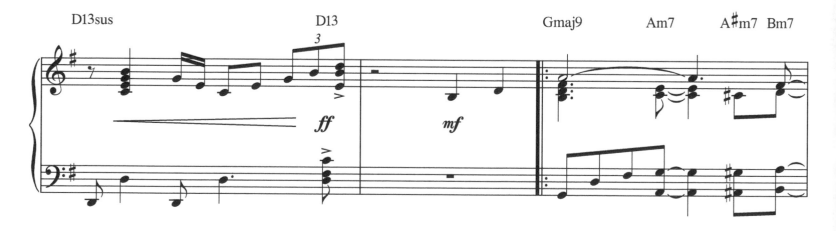

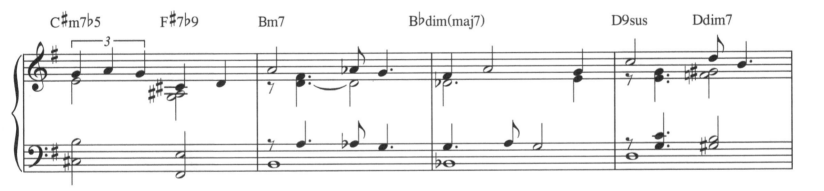

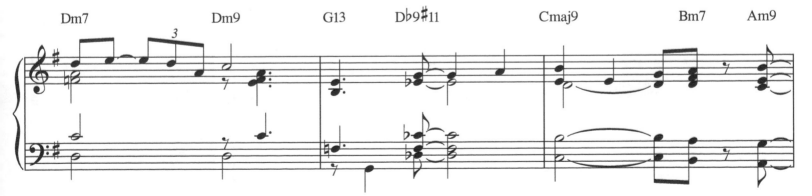

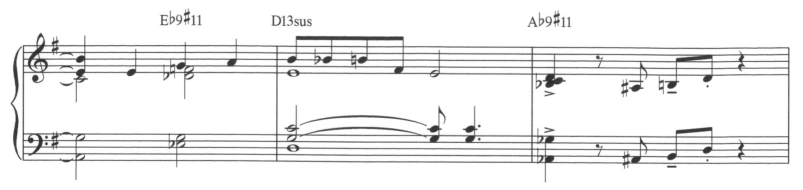

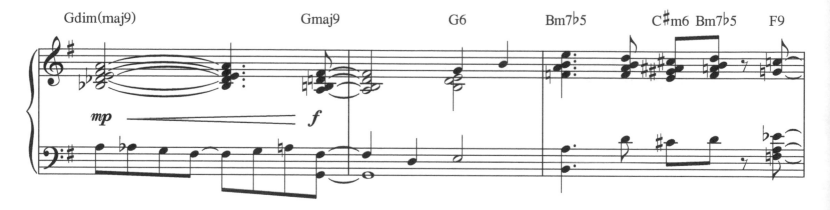

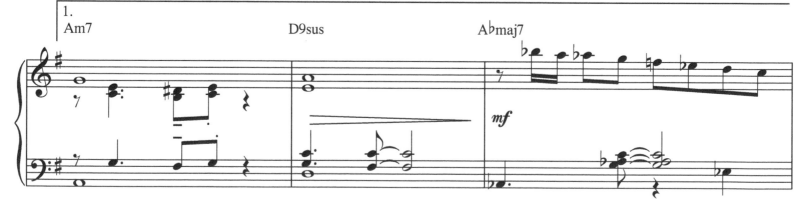

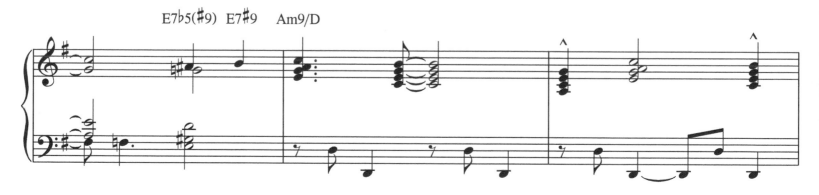

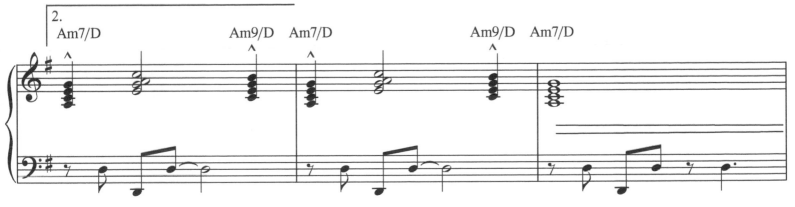

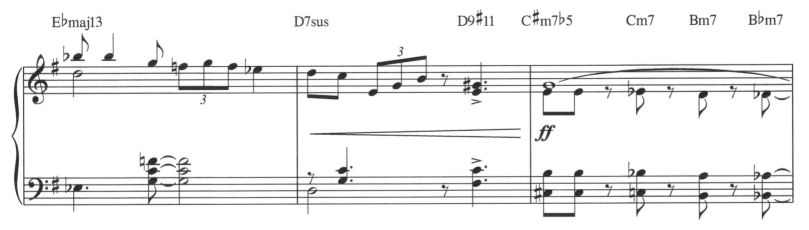

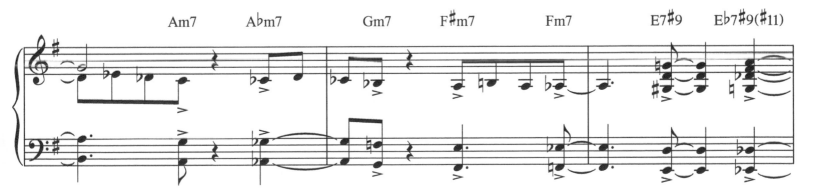

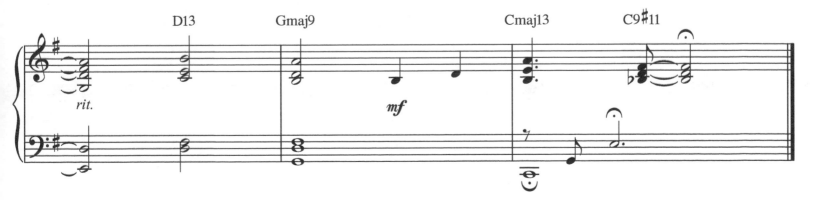

SPEAK LOW

from the Musical Production ONE TOUCH OF VENUS

Words by OGDEN NASH
Music by KURT WEILL

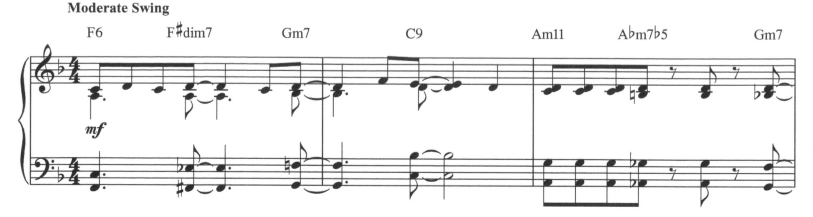

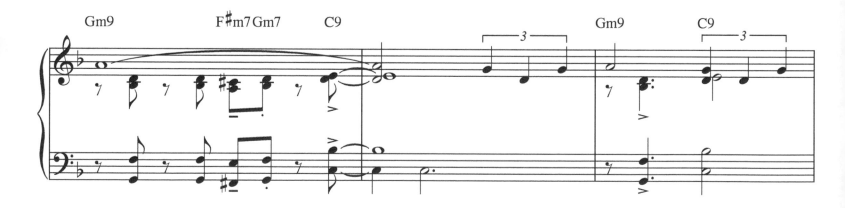

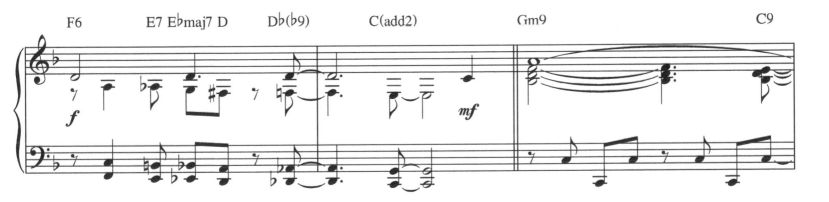

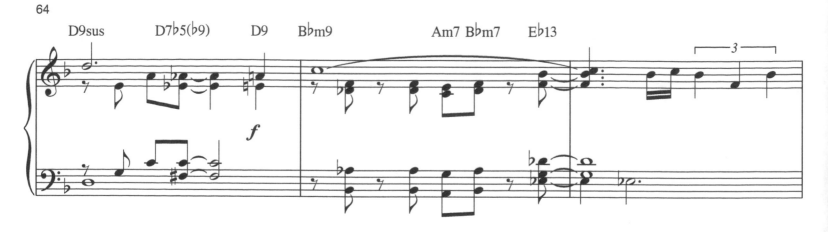

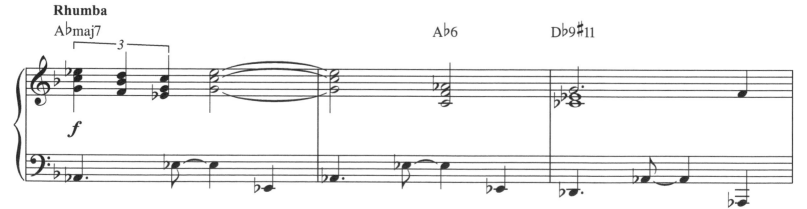

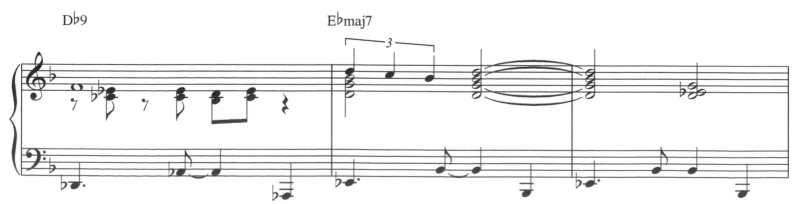

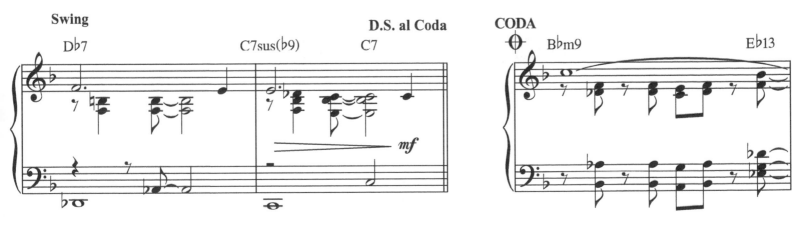

THE SURREY WITH THE FRINGE ON TOP

from OKLAHOMA!

Lyrics by OSCAR HAMMERSTEIN II
Music by RICHARD RODGERS

Swing, not too fast

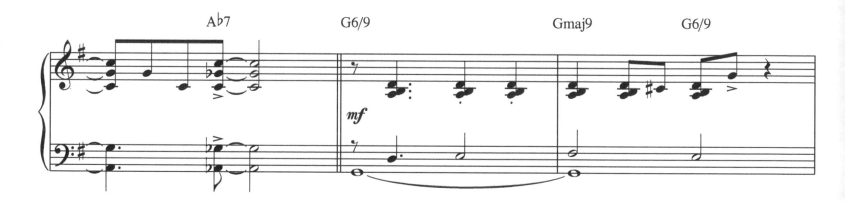

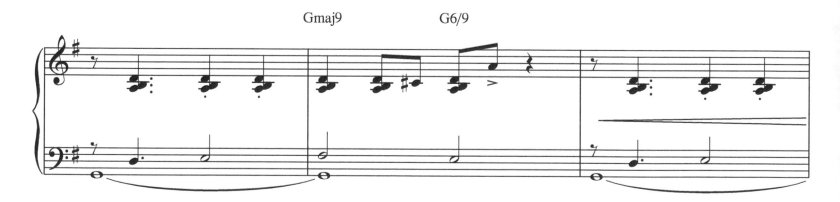

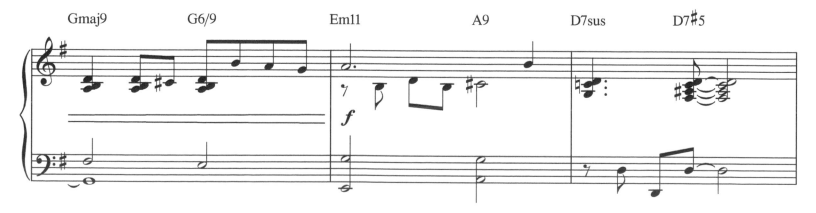

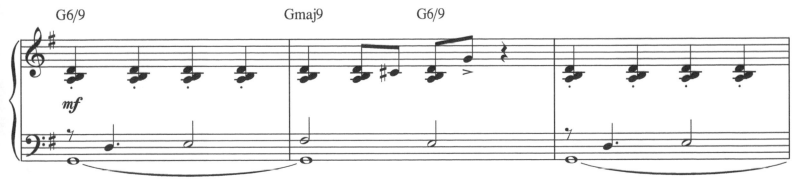

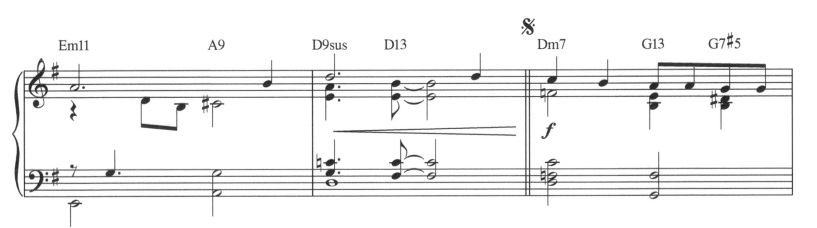

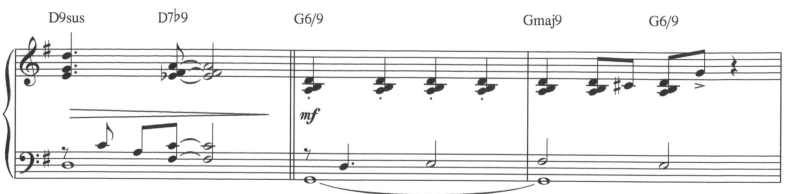

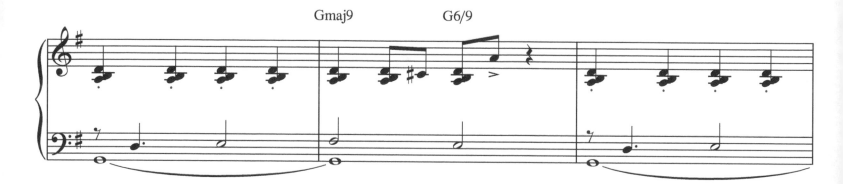

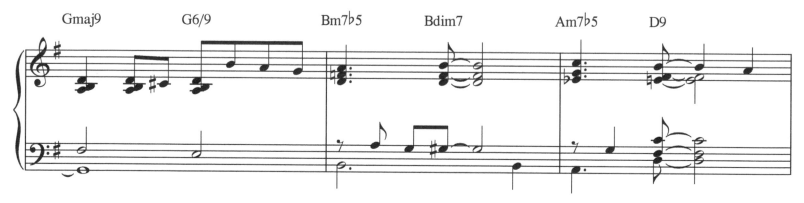

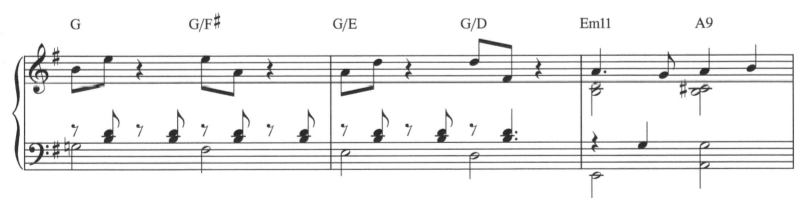

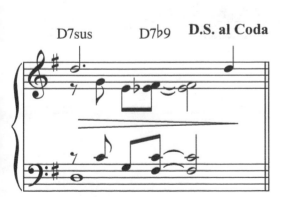

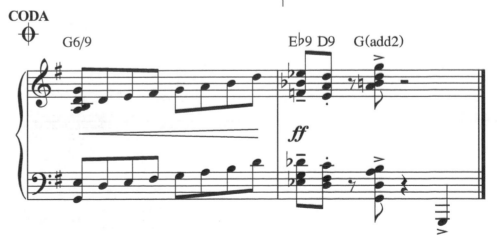

THIS CAN'T BE LOVE

from THE BOYS FROM SYRACUSE

Words by LORENZ HART
Music by RICHARD RODGERS

Bright Swing

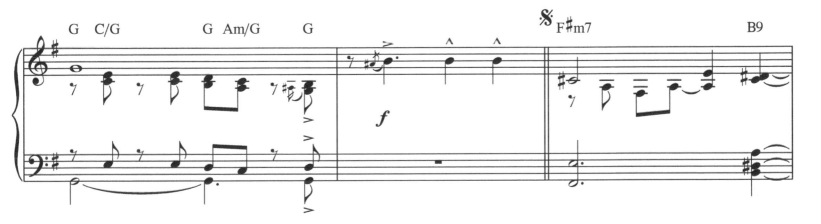

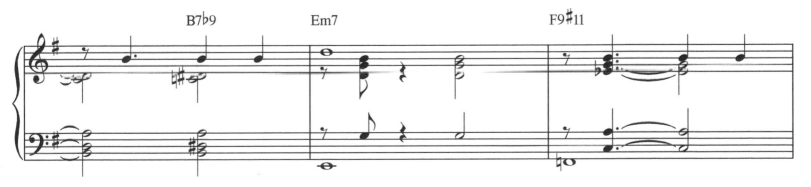

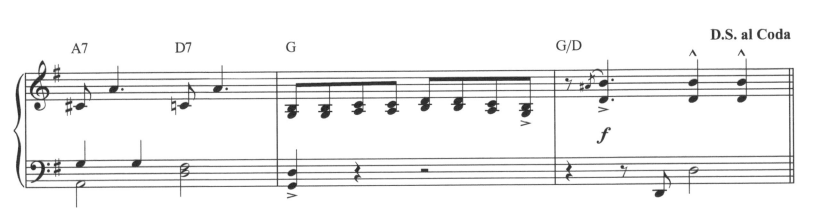

THOU SWELL

from A CONNECTICUT YANKEE

Words by LORENZ HART
Music by RICHARD RODGERS

Moderate Swing

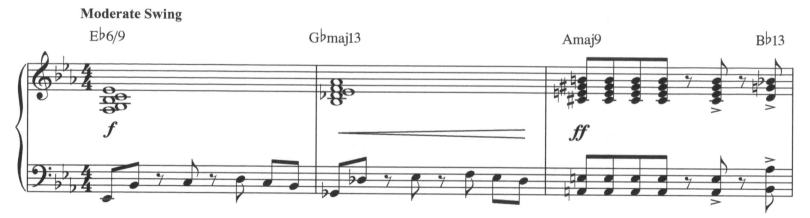

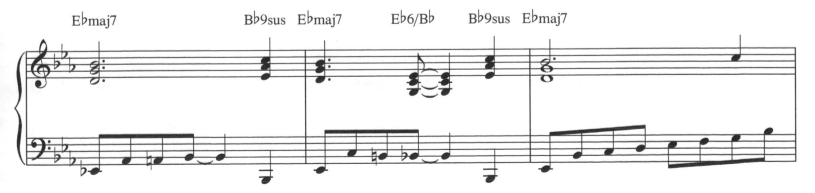

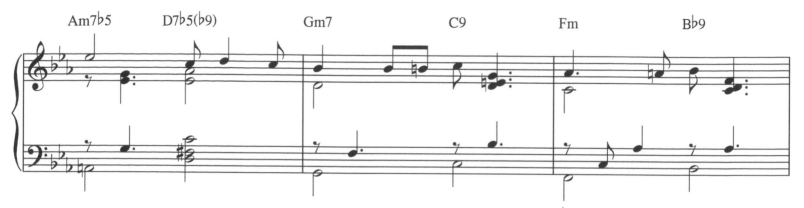

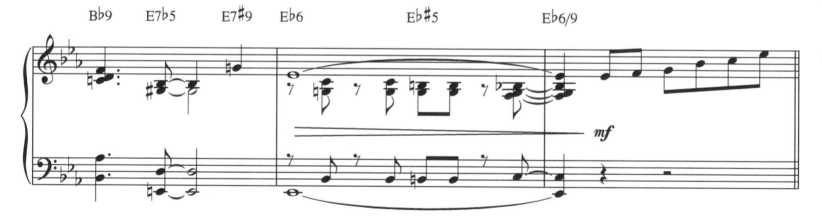

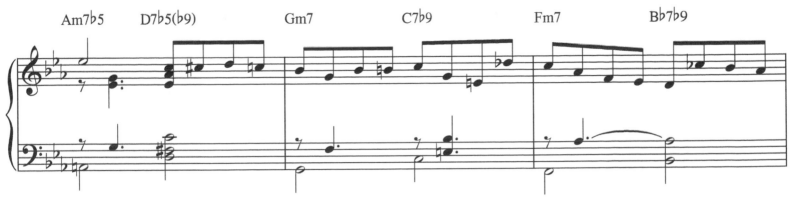

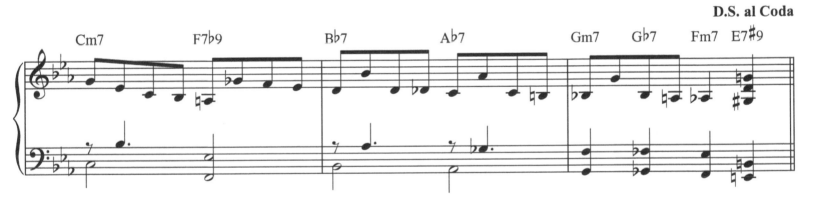

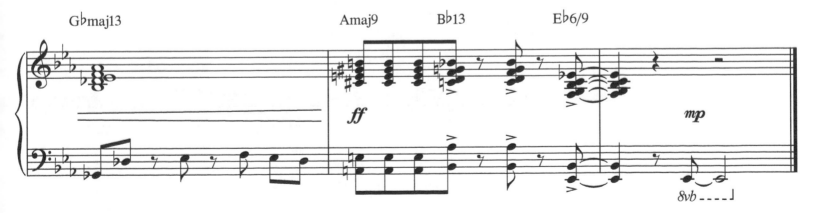

TILL THERE WAS YOU

from Meredith Willson's THE MUSIC MAN

By MERIDETH WILLSON

Flowing

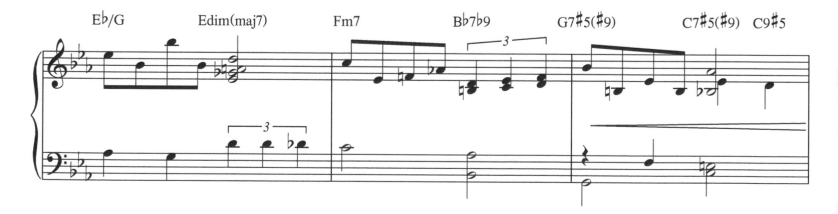

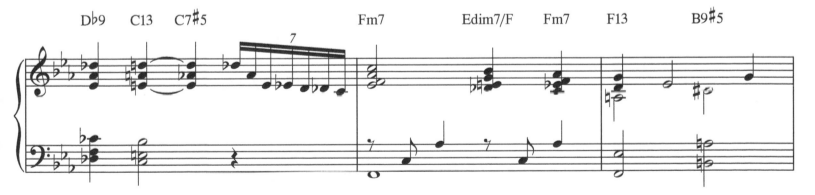

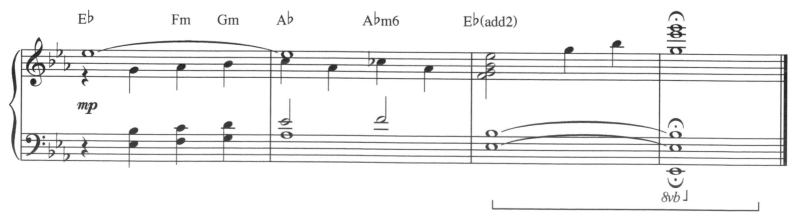

WHO CAN I TURN TO

(When Nobody Needs Me)

from THE ROAR OF THE GREASEPAINT—THE SMELL OF THE CROWD

Words and Music by LESLIE BRICUSSE
and ANTHONY NEWLEY

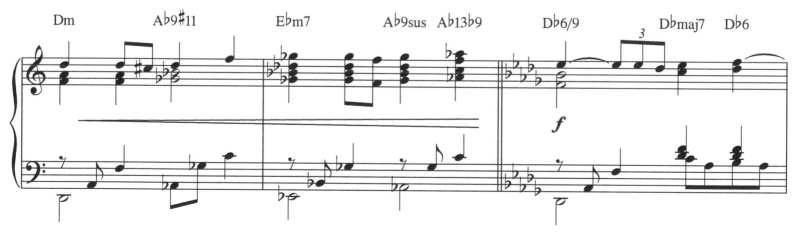

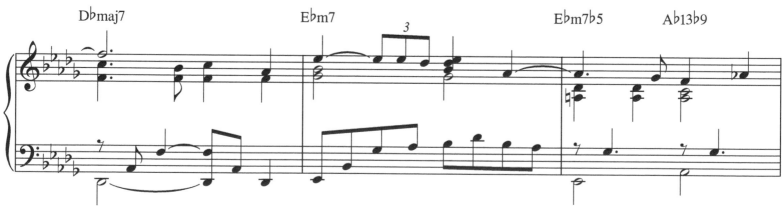

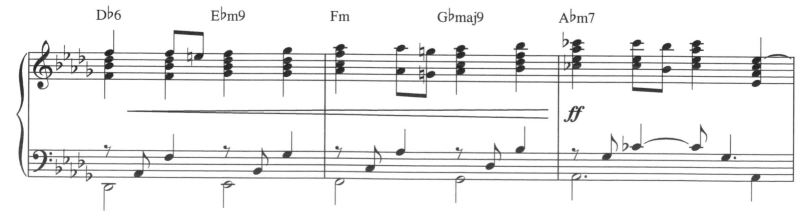

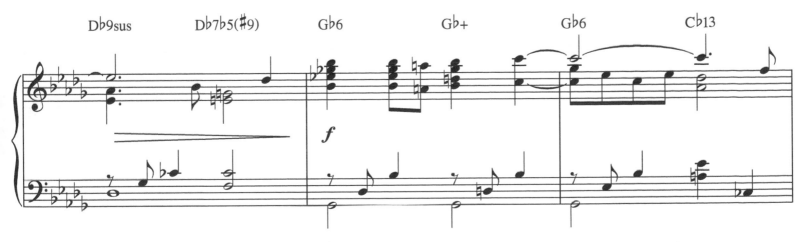

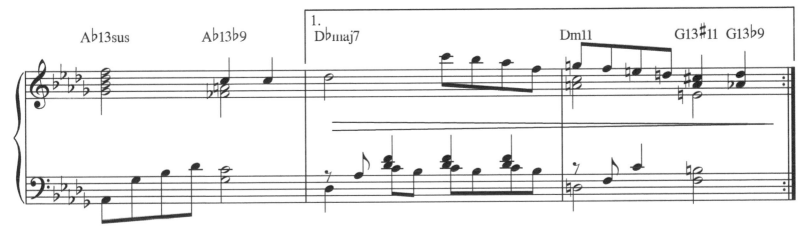

YOU AND THE NIGHT AND THE MUSIC

from REVENGE WITH MUSIC

Words by HOWARD DIETZ
Music by ARTHUR SCHWARTZ

Moderate Latin groove

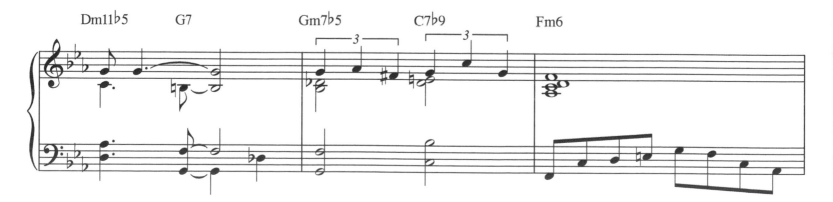

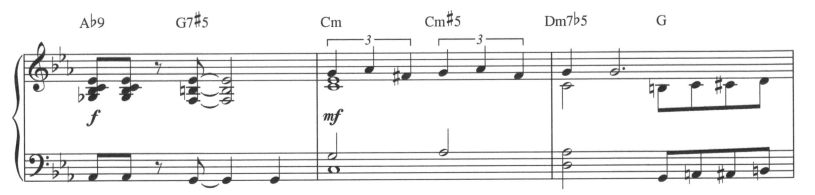

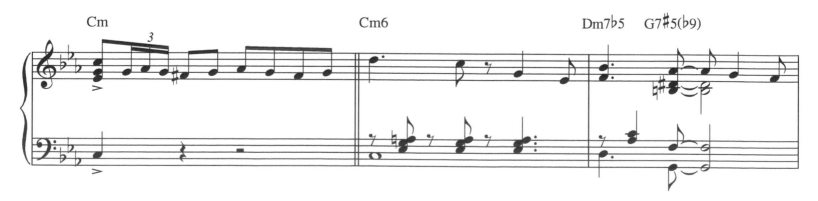

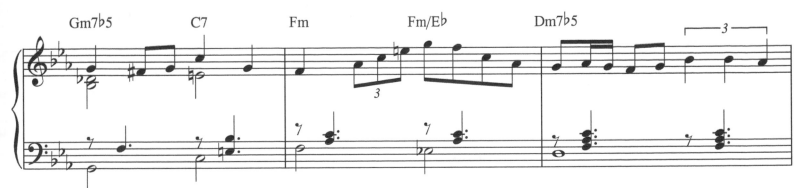

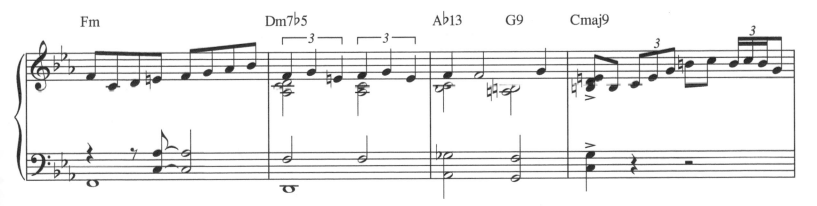

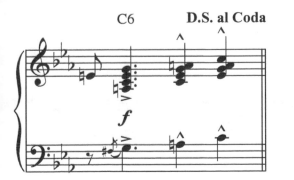

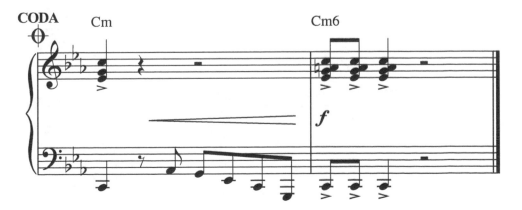

YOU TOOK ADVANTAGE OF ME

from PRESENT ARMS

Words by LORENZ HART
Music by RICHARD RODGERS

Bright Swing

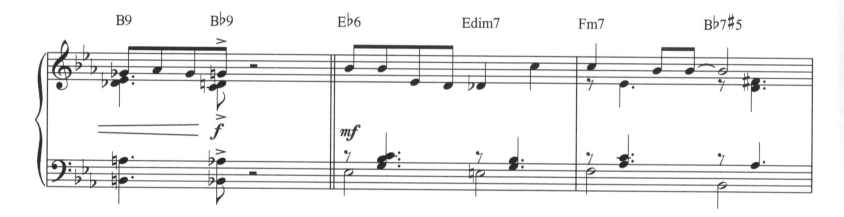

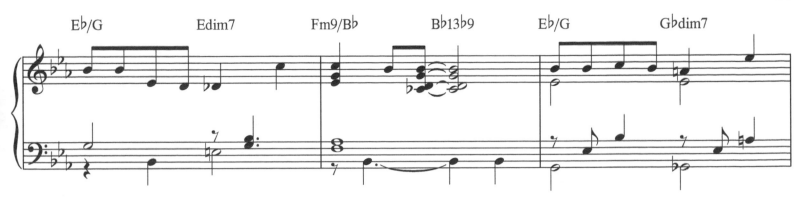

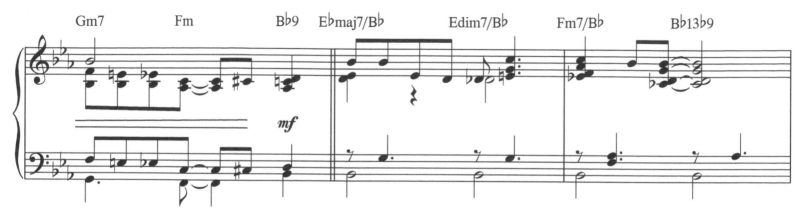

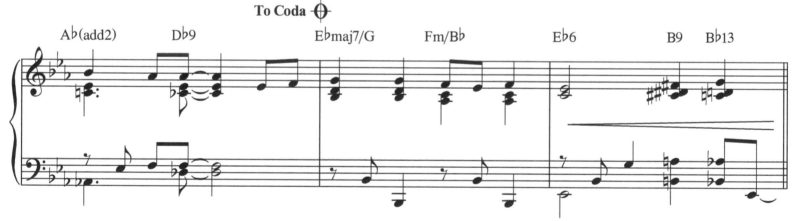

To Coda

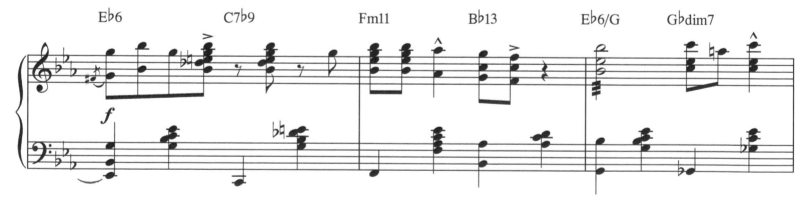

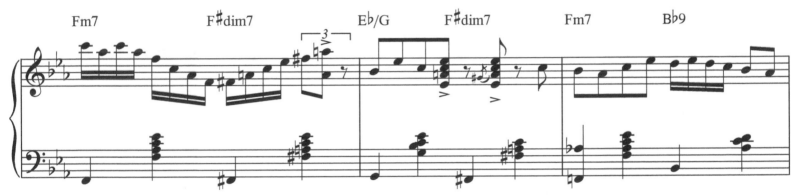

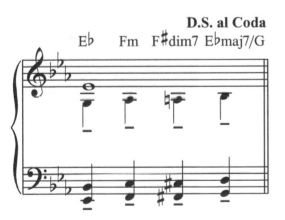

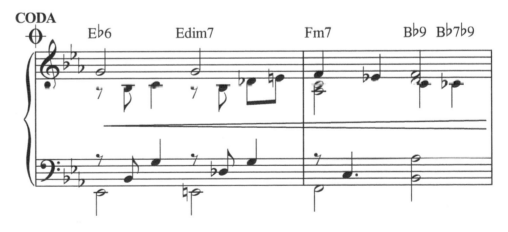

YOUNGER THAN SPRINGTIME

from SOUTH PACIFIC

Lyrics by OSCAR HAMMERSTEIN II
Music by RICHARD RODGERS

Moderately slow, with rubato

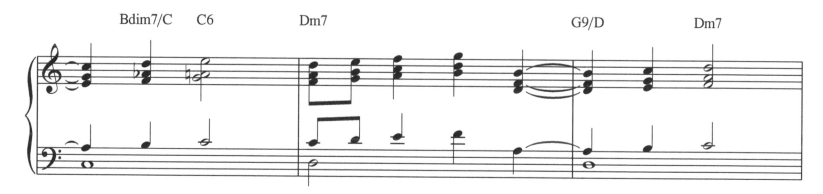

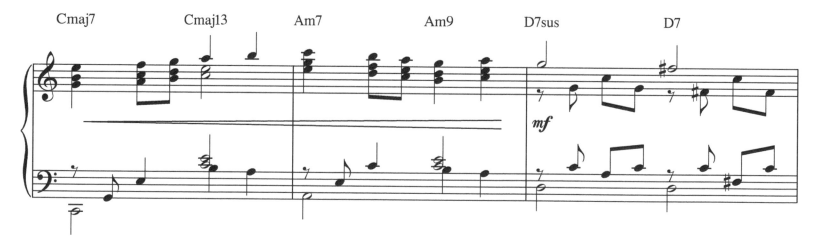

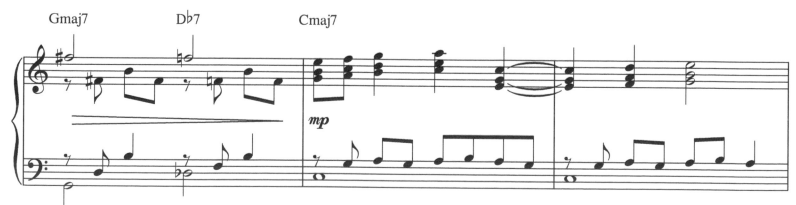

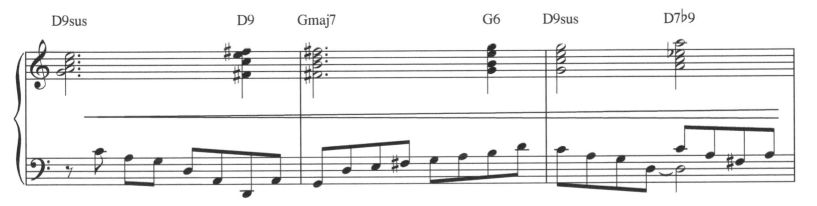

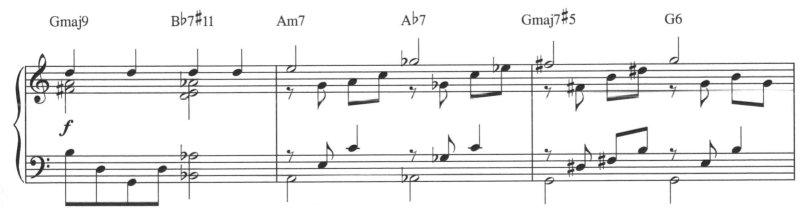

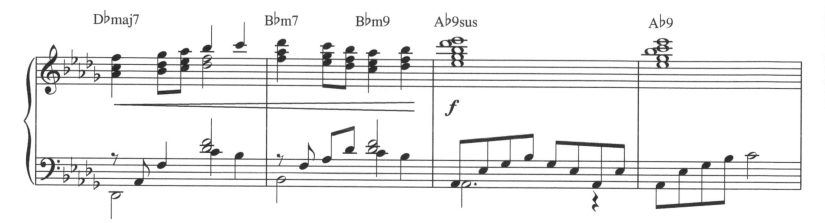

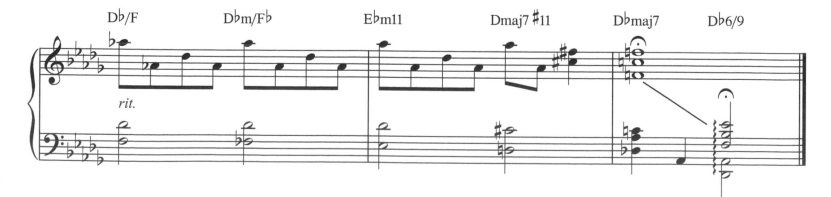

The Best-Selling Jazz Book of All Time Is Now Legal!

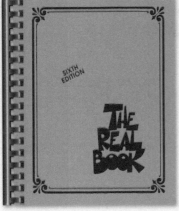

The Real Books are the most popular jazz books of all time. Since the 1970s, musicians have trusted these volumes to get them through every gig, night after night. The problem is that the books were illegally produced and distributed, without any regard to copyright law, or royalties paid to the composers who created these musical masterpieces.

Hal Leonard is very proud to present the first legitimate and legal editions of these books ever produced. You won't even notice the difference, other than all the notorious errors being fixed: the covers and typeface look the same, the song lists are nearly identical, and the price for our edition is even cheaper than the originals!

Every conscientious musician will appreciate that these books are now produced accurately and ethically, benefitting the songwriters that we owe for some of the greatest tunes of all time!

VOLUME 1
00240221	C Edition	$39.99
00240224	B♭ Edition	$39.99
00240225	E♭ Edition	$39.99
00240226	Bass Clef Edition	$39.99
00286389	F Edition	$39.99
00240292	C Edition 6 x 9	$35.00
00240339	B♭ Edition 6 x 9	$35.00
00147792	Bass Clef Edition 6 x 9	$35.00
00451087	C Edition on CD-ROM	$29.99
00200984	Online Backing Tracks: Selections	$45.00
00110604	Book/USB Flash Drive Backing Tracks Pack	$79.99
00110599	USB Flash Drive Only	$50.00

VOLUME 2
00240222	C Edition	$39.99
00240227	B♭ Edition	$39.99
00240228	E♭ Edition	$39.99
00240229	Bass Clef Edition	$39.99
00240293	C Edition 6 x 9	$35.00
00125900	B♭ Edition 6 x 9	$35.00
00451088	C Edition on CD-ROM	$30.99
00125900	The Real Book – Mini Edition	$35.00
00204126	Backing Tracks on USB Flash Drive	$50.00
00204131	C Edition – USB Flash Drive Pack	$79.99

VOLUME 3
00240233	C Edition	$39.99
00240284	B♭ Edition	$39.99
00240285	E♭ Edition	$39.99
00240286	Bass Clef Edition	$39.99
00240338	C Edition 6 x 9	$35.00
00451089	C Edition on CD-ROM	$29.99

VOLUME 4
00240296	C Edition	$39.99
00103348	B♭ Edition	$39.99
00103349	E♭ Edition	$39.99
00103350	Bass Clef Edition	$39.99

VOLUME 5
00240349	C Edition	$39.99
00175278	B♭ Edition	$39.99
00175279	E♭ Edition	$39.99

VOLUME 6
00240534	C Edition	$39.99
00223637	E♭ Edition	$39.99

Also available:
00154230	The Real Bebop Book	$34.99
00240264	The Real Blues Book	$34.99
00310910	The Real Bluegrass Book	$35.00
00240223	The Real Broadway Book	$35.00
00240440	The Trane Book	$22.99
00125426	The Real Country Book	$39.99
00269721	The Real Miles Davis Book C Edition	$24.99
00269723	The Real Miles Davis Book B♭ Edition	$24.99
00240355	The Real Dixieland Book C Edition	$32.50
00294853	The Real Dixieland Book E♭ Edition	$35.00
00122335	The Real Dixieland Book B♭ Edition	$35.00
00240235	The Duke Ellington Real Book	$22.99
00240268	The Real Jazz Solos Book	$30.00
00240348	The Real Latin Book C Edition	$37.50
00127107	The Real Latin Book B♭ Edition	$35.00
00120809	The Pat Metheny Real Book C Edition	$27.50
00252119	The Pat Metheny Real Book B♭ Edition	$24.99
00240358	The Charlie Parker Real Book C Edition	$19.99
00275997	The Charlie Parker Real Book E♭ Edition	$19.99
00118324	The Real Pop Book – Vol. 1	$35.00
00240331	The Bud Powell Real Book	$19.99
00240437	The Real R&B Book C Edition	$39.99
00276590	The Real R&B Book B♭ Edition	$39.99
00240313	The Real Rock Book	$35.00
00240323	The Real Rock Book – Vol. 2	$35.00
00240359	The Real Tab Book	$32.50
00240317	The Real Worship Book	$29.99

THE REAL CHRISTMAS BOOK
00240306	C Edition	$32.50
00240345	B♭ Edition	$32.50
00240346	E♭ Edition	$35.00
00240347	Bass Clef Edition	$32.50
00240431	A-G CD Backing Tracks	$24.99
00240432	H-M CD Backing Tracks	$24.99
00240433	N-Y CD Backing Tracks	$24.99

THE REAL VOCAL BOOK
00240230	Volume 1 High Voice	$35.00
00240307	Volume 1 Low Voice	$35.00
00240231	Volume 2 High Voice	$35.00
00240308	Volume 2 Low Voice	$35.00
00240391	Volume 3 High Voice	$35.00
00240392	Volume 3 Low Voice	$35.00
00118318	Volume 4 High Voice	$35.00
00118319	Volume 4 Low Voice	$35.00

Complete song lists online at www.halleonard.com

Prices, content, and availability subject to change without notice.

0719
318

YOUR FAVORITE MUSIC
ARRANGED FOR PIANO SOLO

 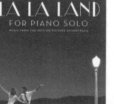   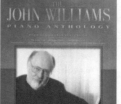 

ARTIST, COMPOSER, TV & MOVIE SONGBOOKS

Adele for Piano Solo
00307585...............................$17.99

The Beatles Piano Solo
00294023...............................$17.99

A Charlie Brown Christmas
00313176...............................$17.99

Paul Cardall – The Hymns Collection
00295925...............................$24.99

Coldplay for Piano Solo
00307637...............................$17.99

Selections from Final Fantasy
00148699...............................$19.99

Alexis Ffrench – The Sheet Music Collection
00345258...............................$19.99

Game of Thrones
00199166...............................$17.99

Hamilton
00345612...............................$19.99

Hillsong Worship Favorites
00303164...............................$12.99

How to Train Your Dragon
00138210...............................$19.99

Elton John Collection
00306040...............................$22.99

La La Land
00283691...............................$14.99

John Legend Collection
00233195...............................$17.99

Les Misérables
00290271...............................$19.99

Little Women
00338470...............................$19.99

Outlander: The Series
00254460...............................$19.99

The Peanuts® Illustrated Songbook
00313178...............................$24.99

Astor Piazzolla – Piano Collection
00285510...............................$17.99

Pirates of the Caribbean – Curse of the Black Pearl
00313256...............................$19.99

Pride & Prejudice
00123854...............................$17.99

Queen
00289784...............................$19.99

John Williams Anthology
00194555...............................$24.99

George Winston Piano Solos
00306822...............................$22.99

 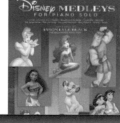   

MIXED COLLECTIONS

Beautiful Piano Instrumentals
00149926...............................$16.99

Best Jazz Piano Solos Ever
00312079...............................$24.99

Best Piano Solos Ever
00242928...............................$19.99

Big Book of Classical Music
00310508...............................$19.99

Big Book of Ragtime Piano
00311749...............................$22.99

Prices, content, and availability subject to change without notice.

Christmas Medleys
00350572...............................$16.99

Disney Medleys
00242588...............................$17.99

Disney Piano Solos
00313128...............................$17.99

Favorite Pop Piano Solos
00312523...............................$16.99

Great Piano Solos
00311273...............................$16.99

The Greatest Video Game Music
00201767...............................$19.99

Disney characters and artwork TM & © 2021 Disney

Most Relaxing Songs
00233879...............................$17.99

Movie Themes Budget Book
00289137...............................$14.99

100 of the Most Beautiful Piano Solos Ever
00102787...............................$29.99

100 Movie Songs
00102804...............................$29.99

Peaceful Piano Solos
00286009...............................$17.99

Piano Solos for All Occasions
00310964...............................$24.99

River Flows in You & Other Eloquent Songs
00123854...............................$17.99

Sunday Solos for Piano
00311272...............................$17.99

Top Hits for Piano Solo
00294635...............................$14.99

HAL•LEONARD®

View songlists online and order from your favorite music retailer at
halleonard.com

0621
195